# THE PERFECT
# WEDDING CAKE

# THE PERFECT
# WEDDING CAKE
## KATE MANCHESTER

STEWART, TABORI & CHANG
NEW YORK

FOREWORD BY SYLVIA WEINSTOCK     PHOTOGRAPHS BY ZEVA OELBAUM

Project editor: Sandra Gilbert
Production: Kim Tyner
Photographer: Zeva Oelbaum
Photography assistant and model: Effie Pavoutsas

Published in 2001 by Stewart, Tabori & Chang
A Company of La Martinière Groupe
115 West 18th Street
New York, NY  10011

Library of Congress Cataloguing-in-Publication Data
Manchester, Kate.
The perfect wedding cake/by Kate Manchester; foreword by Sylvia Weinstock;
photographs by Zeva Oelbaum.
p.cm.
ISBN 1-58479-084-9
1. Wedding cakes. 2. Cake decorating. I. Title.

TX 771.2 .M35 2001
641.8'653--dc21
2001034191

Design by Ivette Montes de Oca

The text of this book was composed in Deepdene. Captions were composed in Trade Gothic.

Printed in Singapore

1 3 5 7 9 10 8 6 4 2
First Printing

# ACKNOWLEDGMENTS

I WOULD LIKE to begin by thanking Sylvia Weinstock for introducing me to the world of fabulous wedding cakes, and by gracing this book with her contributions. Sylvia is one of the many who deserve credit for elevating wedding cakes to their current artistic stature, and her spirit and energy are an inspiration. Betty Van Norstrand, a world-renowned cake decorator and instructor, also deserves a special thanks. Although none of her cakes appear on these pages, almost all of the bakers whose cakes do appear here have studied under Betty, and she is a treasure in the world of decorating.

Zeva Oelbaum is a wonderful photographer and friend, without whom this book never would have happened, nor happened so beautifully. Much credit goes to the unflagging efforts of Sandy Gilbert, the editor from heaven. Her vision, energy, and support kept things on track and on time. To Ivette Montes de Oca for her beautiful style and vision, a very warm thanks.

I would like to extend my gratitude to Gail Watson and Ron Ben-Israel for their early participation in the book. To Toba Garret, thank you for all of your advice, the wonderful recipes, and for introducing me to Rosemary Littman. I wish to extend a heartfelt thanks to Rose Levy Beranbaum for allowing me to include some of her truly perfect wedding cake recipes, and to her assistant Jeannie Bauer who was patient and gracious.

Ellen Bartlett is an artist and cakes are her medium. Thanks for promising one cake and then showing up with six—and wowing us all. Colette Peters is another artist, and a visit to her cake design shop is made more magical by her laughter and whimsical nature.

I must thank François Payard for the fabulous *croquembouche*—and for a magnificent lunch. Ellen Baumwoll is a lovely person and talented, too; thank you for answering my questions, sharing your recipes, and introducing me to Joe Gilmartin. Thanks to my oldest friend Mary Ann Van Degna and her wonderful husband Bob for their gracious hospitality, wedding dresses, and for introducing me to Dana at Scrumptions. And finally to David, for your patience and understanding, but mostly for giving me the time I needed.

To all of those old friends and new friends who participated in this book, who gave me their time, made suggestions and introductions, answered questions, and brought me their vision of wedding cake perfection—a warm and heartfelt thanks.

# CONTENTS

# FOREWORD

WHEN ALL IS SAID AND DONE, what do we remember about the wedding? Luscious flowers, beautiful dress, stunning wedding cake? Many brides have told me that, years down the road, the cake is one of their strongest memories—and hopefully it's a pleasant one.

In olden days, sweet cakes were only for the rich; sugar was an expensive ingredient. As time progressed, many more people could afford wedding cakes. The cake came to symbolize the sharing of prosperity, sweetness, and love with the wedding guests, as well as with the bride and groom.

For me, the challenge of designing a cake appropriate to the season, the décor, and the personality of the bridal couple became a passion. Gone is the inedible, dry stereotype of a wedding cake. Now, we can find beautiful cakes that are delicious to eat—be they chocolate with chocolate mousse, or yellow butter cake with fresh lemon curd and seasonal berries, each coated with a light, creamy buttercream. What a change! And almost anything can be used to decorate a cake today: sugar flowers—confections on a confection—in all colors of the spectrum, even a marzipan model of the groom's dog—anything goes, as long as it's delicious!

May that special day live in memory as a highlight in your life.

—*Sylvia Weinstock*

# WEDDING CAKE LORE AND HISTORY

The wedding cake is one of the oldest and most beloved traditions of today's wedding ceremony. Bread and cakes have been associated with weddings throughout history, often representing the bride's fertility. Ancient Romans shared a plain bread made from wheat or barley, salt, and water during their wedding ceremonies. The bread was broken over the bride's head by the groom, symbolizing both his dominance over her and the taking of her virginity. Later, this custom evolved to include the bridesmaids covering the head of the bride with a white cloth prior to the breaking of the bread. Some believe that this practice led to another tradition: the wearing of the bridal veil.

In medieval England, sweet rolls were piled high between the bride and groom during the wedding celebration. The couple would try to kiss over the top without tumbling the rolls; a successful embrace was supposed to ensure a life of happiness with many children.

During the reign of King Charles II, it is rumored that a French chef visiting London observed this cake-piling ceremony. Upon his return to France, he transformed the pile of sweet rolls into today's classic French wedding cake—the magnificent *croquembouche*.

Many argue that the wedding-cake tradition as we know it started in Great Britain. Simon R. Charsley writes in his book *Wedding Cakes and Cultural History* that the earliest

recorded British recipe for a wedding cake (dated 1665) was, in fact, a pie. Eventually, the customary British wedding cake became a fruitcake.

The wedding cake tradition has spread around the world, and has been adapted in a variety of forms into many cultures. In India, for example, the wedding cake is present at Christian ceremonies. However, most of India is Hindu, and wedding feasts in that tradition feature an abundant variety of sweets but no wedding cake per se.

At Chinese wedding banquets, the food served is symbolic of happiness, longevity, and fertility. Dessert features a sweet, steamed bread filled with lotus paste, which represents fruitfulness, but no wedding cake as we know it. In Mexico, traditional wedding cakes are small pastries made from flour, butter, and almonds. The pastries are wrapped in brightly colored tissue so that the guests can take them home.

The classic style of a wedding cake, with successively smaller, stacked tiers, is believed to have been inspired by the spire of the fourteenth-century Saint Bride's Church in the city of London. Although the church had been in existence for centuries, the multitiered wedding cake first appeared at nineteenth-century royal weddings. An 1840 edition of the *London Times* reported that Queen Victoria's wedding cake was more than nine feet in circumference, with a second tier arising from a plateau supported by two pedestals. The second tier was not a cake at all, but a sugar sculpture of the mythical Britannia gazing upon the royal couple exchanging their vows. Also adorning the massive cake were sculpted turtle doves, representing purity and innocence, and a dog, representing faithfulness and loyalty.

Since early nineteenth-century bakers lacked the engineering skill to stack cakes without the tiers crushing one another, it was customary for the bottom or base tier to be cake, while the top part of the cake consisted of sugar sculptures, spun sugar, or faux cakes made of pure sugar. It was not until 1870 that the wedding cake became an actual tiered cake, and not until twenty years later that tiers of cake were separated by columns.

Like the bride's dress, the classic wedding cake is white. The white icing originally symbolized virginal attributes, and a link was made between the whiteness of the cake and the purity of the bride. However, status was another reason for the cake to be white. During Victorian times, the finer wedding-cake ingredients were scarce. White icing revealed that only the most expensive, refined white sugar was used, instead of the less expensive and more common brown sugar. The whiter the cake, the more affluent the family.

Although the wedding cake is still a prominent part of the wedding ceremony, many couples no longer opt for a traditional cake. Today's cakes may reflect a couple's dreams or their ethnic heritage. Cakes can range from understated to elegant to wildly imaginative. The modern couple is no longer limited by societal rules and scarcity of materials; their cake can be anything and everything they desire.

PAGE 12: A modern twist on a classic French wedding cake, the delicious individual *croquembouche*, by François Payard of Payard Patisserie. OPPOSITE: This pretty fondant cake is covered with chartreuse viburnum, pink tulips, and blue hyacinth, all made out of gum paste. Created by Ellen Bartlett of Cakes To Remember.

YOUR WEDDING

CA

# K E

1

Once upon a time, a three-tiered, white-frosted sponge cake with a plastic bride-and-groom cake topper was the standard for almost every wedding. I see, in faded, black-and-white photographs, that my own parents had this very cake at their wedding—complete with the plastic couple on top. The easily forgotten slices of this cake were to be cut and served just before the guests

made their exit, an act representing both the couple's togetherness and the end of the wedding celebration.

Today's wedding cake, however, is more likely to be a showstopping centerpiece, one that actually tastes good and is served as dessert, sometimes long before the end of the celebration. Gone are the days of a white wedding cake made up of three tiers and covered in royal icing. Modern wedding cake creations are veritable works of art that complement the bridal couple's wedding style. The sky is the limit when it comes to dreaming up your confectionary fantasy.

Displayed for all the guests to see throughout the wedding

reception, the wedding cake is as important as the flowers and the dress, and how it looks and tastes matters now more than ever. The cake is a reflection of the couple's style and good taste, and the cutting of the cake still symbolizes the couple's first act as a married couple.

Whether you consider yourselves to be a traditional or modern couple, your sense of style will dictate the kind of wedding and wedding cake you should have. You don't have to stick to tradition when it comes to your cake. Design a cake that befits you, whether that's tiers of cupcakes or individual miniature wedding cakes. Before designing the cake of your dreams, determine the date, location, and number of guests attending your wedding; and decide on your bridal bouquet and the style of your dress.

Once you've gotten this far into the planning, your wedding

OPPOSITE: Classic white fondant is the perfect palette for many decorating styles. Here, soft yellow roses, calla lilies, and ivy fashioned from gum paste make an elegant adornment. Created by Michelle Buhigian of Something Sweet by Michelle.

# WINTER

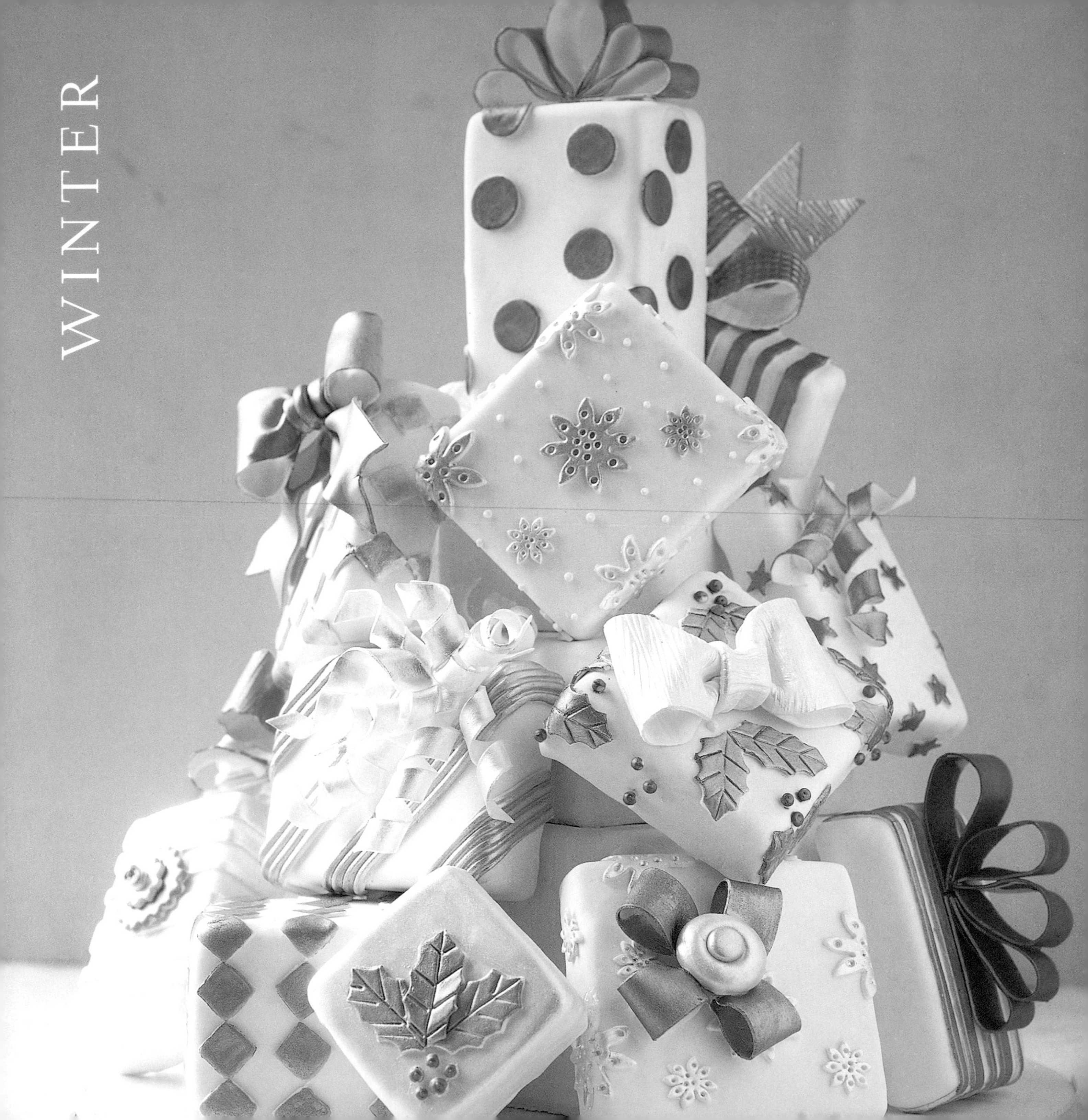

# SUMMER

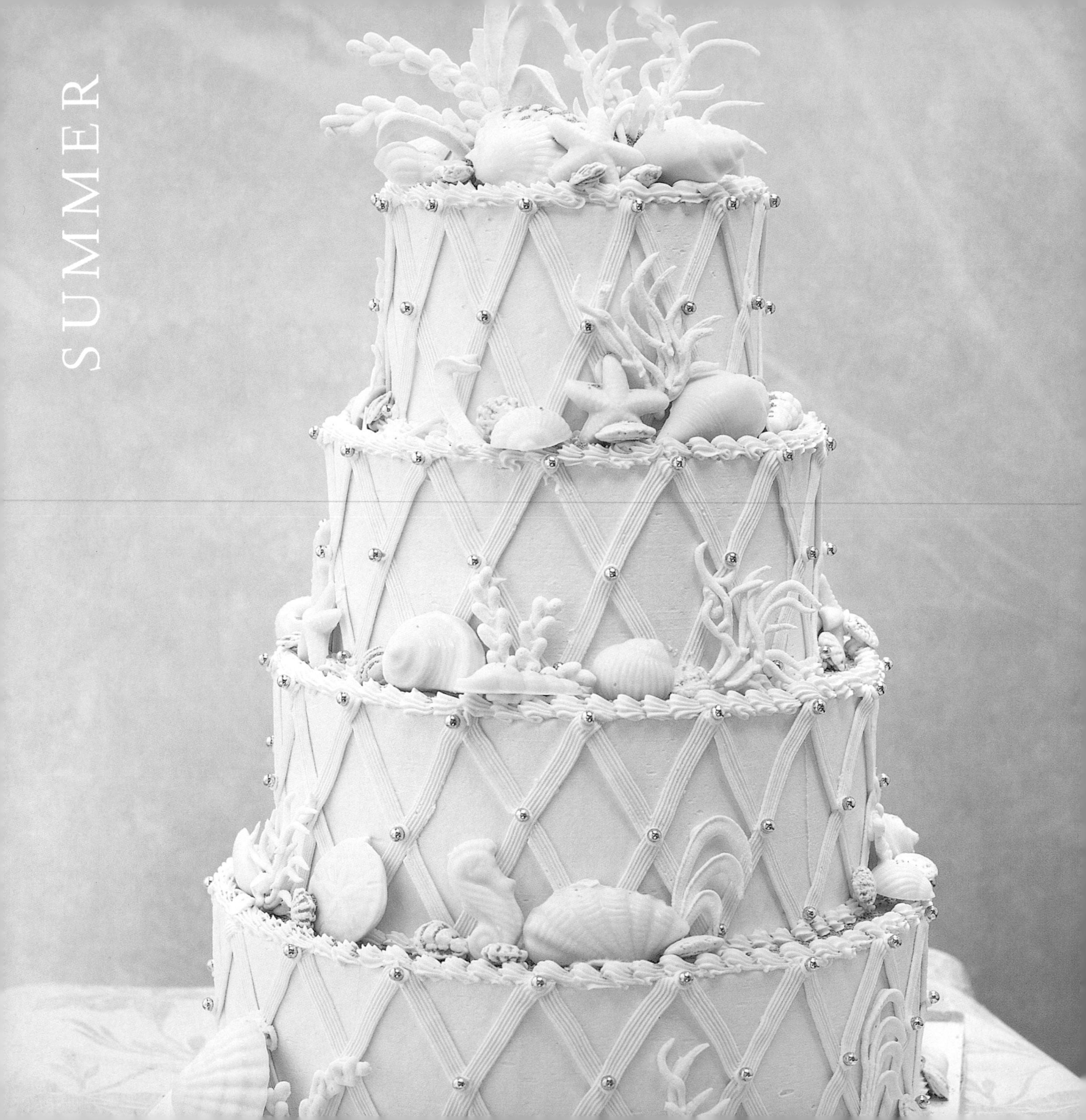

will have developed a certain style or theme. You want to have a cake that is in sync with the character of your wedding. When you have an idea of these particulars, you can begin to ask yourself other questions. Is there a cake you have always dreamed about? Is your wedding reception inside or outside? In which season will it occur? Will your wedding be simple and elegant, or a grand, lavish affair? What day of the week will it be, and what time of day? Is it an intimate second or third wedding? Is the reception room an ornate ballroom or your parents' backyard? What colors are your flowers and the bridesmaids' dresses?

In addition to the look of the cake, begin to think about the flavors you and your soon-to-be spouse enjoy the most. Meanwhile, keep in mind the decisions you have made. If you both love frozen chocolate mousse cake with whipped cream icing, it may be the perfect option if your wedding takes place during the winter months. Serving this kind of cake to your guests in the backyard of your parents' home on a steamy August afternoon is still an option, but only if your parents have a freezer large enough to accommodate a wedding cake and if you don't mind your guests seeing the cake whiz from freezer to table.

As for the baker, don't feel obligated to let your caterer make your cake. Of course, if your caterer employs a superb wedding-cake baker, you may want to save money by using him or her. Ordinarily, opting to go with an outside baker will be a bit more expensive, but the results are generally well worth it. Seek out a baker in your area whose cake designs thrill you, and

find out if they can work within your time frame.

Many wedding-cake bakers recommend you book the date a minimum of three to six months in advance, but as some bakers are booked up to a year in advance with cake orders, more time is acceptable and encouraged. Remember that there are many more weddings during the late spring, summer, and early fall. During these particularly busy times for your baker, try to give them extra advance notice of your wedding date. You won't be required to decide on the particulars of your dream cake yet, but you do want to reserve the date with the baker.

**PAGES 20-21:** Stacks of fondant-wrapped gift box cakes (left) placed on each table make festive centerpieces for a winter holiday wedding. Created by Colette Peters of Colette's Cakes. This delightful cake (right), covered in a cascade of sugar blossoms and butterflies, will make every guest think of spring. Created by Gail Watson Custom Cakes.

**PAGES 22-23:** Pale creamy buttercream, silver dragées, and white chocolate seashells set the stage for a summer wedding by the sea (left). Created by Scrumptions. This elaborate fall harvest cake (right) is shaped like a basket and brimming with fruits, leaves, and flowers, all fashioned by hand in gum paste. Created by Ellen Bartlett of Cakes To Remember.

**OPPOSITE:** Toba Garrett is a skilled pastry chef, a talented cake-decorating instructor, and the owner of her own business, Cake Decorating by Toba. She shows off her intricate lace work on this splendid cake, which is draped in fondant swags.

# TY
### OF CAKES

PES 2

The rules have changed, and while no reception is complete without a wedding cake, people today are willing to do things a little differently than tradition once dictated. Many of us still picture a wedding cake as a three- or four-tiered design, with the tiers stacked or separated by columns. Even this classic style can be successfully updated. For instance, many bakers change the

traditional round layers to square, oval, or even heart-shaped tiers.

Some bridal couples are moving even further away from convention and opting for whimsical cakes that have personal significance. The cake, a great sculpting medium, can become a replica of the couple's new home or a beautiful vase full of colorful flowers. It can be transformed into a fantastic Fabergé egg or built into a leaning tower that looks like it's about to topple over. The possibilities are virtually endless.

Miniature wedding cakes, iced and decorated with as much care as a grand cake, are turning up at many weddings as individual desserts in place of the traditional cake slice. Other couples are giving beautifully boxed miniatures to guests as wedding favors. Though delicate and beautiful, these diminutive confections can be a costly alternative to a larger wedding cake,

and many bakers refuse to do them. Imagine baking, icing, and decorating a tiny cake for each of your 250 wedding guests!

Another popular alternative to the traditional large wedding cake is a group of centerpiece cakes that serve as both decoration and dessert at each table. These smaller wedding cakes are designed to feed ten to twelve people, or however many guests will be seated at each table. They can all be decorated as identical cakes, or they can all be different. The bride and groom may consider having their own small wedding cake placed at the main table, and following the cake-cutting

OPPOSITE: Elegant whimsy is the only way to describe this amazing creation by Colette Peters. She has bejewelled this cake with brightly colored fondant, gumpaste flowers and ribbons, gold dragées, and a dusting of edible gold.

ceremony, the waitstaff could come to each table to cut, plate, and serve the cakes. Many bakers are more receptive to doing a series of smaller cakes, which are much less labor-intensive than miniatures, and they may welcome the opportunity to show off ten different wedding cakes instead of one large cake.

Tiers of brightly iced and decorated cupcakes stacked on graduated cake stands will give the illusion of a tiered cake, and are a fun alternative at a less formal wedding. Cupcakes can be covered in individual or bouquets of flowers to suit any season or color scheme, and unlike miniature cakes, only the top needs decorating. All the children at your reception will be thrilled, and your waitstaff will be too. Plating a cupcake requires much less effort than cutting and plating cake slices!

For a holiday wedding, stacks of fondant-covered, brightly ribboned gift box cakes set on each guest table make a festive alternative to a tiered cake. Holiday cakes tend to have a white theme, often with touches of gold or silver.

While serving a cake at your wedding is still a tradition, the confections that are turning up at receptions are creative variations on an age-old theme. The creative cakes on these pages are representative of the spirit of today's wedding style.

**LEFT:** Cupcakes, stacked and tiered, are a charming alternative to the traditional large wedding cake. These individual confections, here adorned with marzipan roses, are enjoyed by guests in place of a slice of cake. Created by Cheryl Kleinman Cakes.

**RIGHT:** Delight your wedding guests with several small cakes on each table. This gift box–shaped cake serves four and has a surprise inside—the interior is creamy cheesecake. The wrapping, ribbon, and pearls are white chocolate. Created by Susan Morgan of Elegant Cheese Cakes.

**PAGES 32-33:** Cake design takes its inspiration from many sources. The refinement of Wedgwood china is reflected in the stately grace of this creation by Cheryl Kleinman Cakes (left). Ellen Bartlett of Cakes To Remember created this cake (right) to reflect the bridal party's yellow and blue dresses and bouquets.

# CA

## FLAVORS

## FILLINGS

# KE
## ICINGS

3

After all the care you will take in choosing a wonderful menu for your guests, why not serve them a dessert that is both attractive to look at and delicious to eat? In fact, every baker I have talked to insists that wedding cakes

are supposed to be the delicious dessert after a spectacular meal. Your guests will be looking at your wedding cake for a good part of the day, and if it's a gorgeous creation they will be fantasizing about what it tastes like. Most people love dessert, and even if they don't ordinarily eat it, they will be so enticed by your gorgeous cake that even the most disciplined won't be able to resist a piece.

There is one golden rule for a delicious wedding cake: Always use fresh ingredients. You should insist that only the highest quality eggs, sweet butter, and sugar go into your cake. Also, try to use seasonal fruits, as they are likely to be the most flavorful ones available. Using top-quality ingredients will make a noticeable difference in how your cake tastes.

Since your wedding day will be a long one, punctuated by alcohol and many different kinds of foods, your guests' palettes may become a little dulled by the time your cake is served. The flavors you choose for your cake can and should be bolder and stronger than you might think.

A cake is constructed in layers. Customarily, three layers of cake and two layers of filling make up one cake tier. First, one layer of cake is brushed with some kind of liquid wash, such as a fruit syrup or liqueur, to keep it moist. Next, the filling tops the layer. Then, another layer of cake sits atop the filling.

The whole process is repeated until you have one tier ready to be iced. The process is repeated again with the cake or cakes that will sit on the base cake. The cake tiers are then iced and covered. A lengthy process, indeed, in which all elements need to work well together.

The cake, filling, and icing should all complement one another. Pairing a smooth lemon curd with a chocolate cake would be an insult to the cake as well as to the lemon curd. The best way to find a delicious combination is to taste, so concoct some ideas, then plan a time with your baker when you and your fiancé can sample different kinds of cakes and fillings. A good baker will always agree to and welcome a tasting session. Remember to go for a tender, moist cake, and bold flavors in fillings and icings.

OPPOSITE: A rich dark-chocolate layer cake (top left) with a creamy chocolate-mousse filling is covered with poured-chocolate ganache. The slice is served with a raspberry puree and fresh raspberries. A moist buttercream cake (bottom right) is filled with tart lemon and cool raspberry mousses, then iced with a refreshing lemon buttercream. The edible flowers by Meadowsweets make a beautiful garnish.

PAGE 39: This delicious white cake created by Ron Ben-Israel Cakes is enhanced with blackberry filling and white-chocolate mousseline, then iced with a smooth buttercream and covered in pink rolled fondant.

Sample cakes that are iced with buttercream and ones covered with fondant or marzipan so you will know the difference.

The cake flavors and fillings should reflect your tastes, and often you and your partner will share the same taste—or at least be able to compromise on a combination of flavors that satisfies both of you. There is an alternative, however, if you cannot decide. If you are serving any kind of tiered cake, you can have a different cake and filling for each tier: chocolate cake and mocha mousse filling for one cake, yellow sponge cake with strawberry mousse for the next tier, carrot cake with cream cheese filling for the third. When the different kinds of slices come to the table, there are lots of tastings and trading of slices, which can make for great conversation and fun at the table.

## FILLINGS

Some of the more common fillings for cakes today are buttercream, flavored mousses, pastry cream, whipped cream, ganache, and fruit jam.

## FILLINGS

BUTTERCREAM can be made with either egg yolks or whites. The egg yolks or whites are combined with copious amounts of hot sugar and sweet butter. Each concoction will have a slightly different taste and texture, but will be equally delicious. An egg-yolk buttercream, often called a "classic" buttercream, is very rich and creamy in texture. An egg-white or "meringue" buttercream has a silken taste and texture. Some bakers like to use the egg-yolk buttercream as a filling and the meringue buttercream as icing.

CUSTARD OR PASTRY CREAM is a delicate, milk- and egg-based filling. Although delectable, it doesn't work well in cakes that will sit for a long time at a warm temperature. Whipped-cream fillings are equally luscious but also need to be kept chilled.

GANACHE is a luxurious combination of chocolate and heavy cream that can be used as either a filling or an icing, depending on the proportions of the ingredients.

MOUSSES OR MOUSSELINES are a delicious alternative to buttercream. They can be flavored with fruit or dark or white chocolate. A cake filled with mousse can be frozen and will taste delicious even if it is not thawed completely at serving time.

FRESH FRUIT complements many cake flavors and styles. Between layers of yellow cake, fresh raspberries or strawberries tucked into a chocolate or lemon mousse add fresh taste and bright color to every slice. If you intend to use fresh fruit, be sure that the fruits you choose will be available and ripe on your wedding day.

# ICINGS AND CAKE COVERINGS

BUTTERCREAM icing is traditionally made from egg whites, butter, and sugar. The sugar is heated, then added to the egg whites very slowly. Later, the butter is added bit by bit. Buttercream takes flavor and color very well, may be used for bordering and piping, and tastes delicious on most cakes. Buttercream icing can be refrigerated, but because of its high butter content it is not recommended if you will be serving your cake in very hot or humid weather. By varying the recipe slightly, buttercream makes a great cake filling.

FONDANT (OR ROLLED FONDANT) is a very popular covering for wedding cakes. It is made from glucose or corn syrup and shortening, and holds up well on a warm day. A cake covered in fondant has a smooth, satiny look.The fondant drapes and clings beautifully to the cake. It will seal in the freshness of a cake for several days and lends itself to ornate decoration. But, a cake covered in fondant cannot be refrigerated and will therefore limit the kinds of fillings you will be able to use.

MARZIPAN is similar to fondant in the way it looks. Made from almond paste, it tastes delicious and is often used for modeling fruits or sculpting figures to decorate cakes.

Marzipan can be used to cover cakes, although it forms a hard crust. Cutting a cake covered in marzipan may cause crumbling because of the crust, and so it works better between cake layers or molded into forms for decoration. A marzipan-covered cake can be refrigerated, but it is not recommended. If the cake is not covered and sealed carefully, moisture from the refrigerator can form droplets on the surface of the cake and ruin its look.

ROLLED CHOCOLATE most often refers to chocolate fondant; sometimes called chocolate plastic or plastique. Bakers make it by warming chocolate and tempering it with small amounts of glycerine or corn syrup. While similar to fondant in that it can be colored, rolled, and draped, its taste is superior— pure chocolate.

ROYAL ICING is pure white and generally used for delicate piping or lace work. It must be kept at room temperature, and dries to a very hard consistency, which makes it a natural medium for decorating. Royal icing does not hold up well in humidity and cannot be refrigerated. Therefore, it is not recommended for icing an entire cake.

It's possible that the fillings you select for your cake may be limited by your choice of decorations. If a cake requires hours of decoration, which translates to hours of sitting at room temperature before it gets to your reception, it may not be possible to use fresh mousses, or whipped or pastry creams as fillings, because they tend to break down quickly. These cakes (and cakes that are too big to be refrigerated) can be filled with ganache or certain kinds of buttercream.

## ICINGS AND CAKE COVERINGS

Before you sit down with your cake baker, you may have an image in your mind of what you want your cake to look like. Each cake covering has different attributes and advantages, and it's important to know the differences among them before deciding what will work best for your cake. More often than not, a cake that has a porcelain-smooth, flawless, or rounded edge is covered in rolled fondant, marzipan, or rolled chocolate. A smooth, flat finish can be achieved using buttercream, although it takes a skilled and patient hand.

Often a cake that is covered in fondant or marzipan will be iced first. Fondant looks beautiful as a cake covering, but many people don't enjoy eating it because it is very sweet.

Now that you are familiar with the basic elements of cake construction, you can begin thinking about all the delicious cakes and flavor combinations that appeal to you. Choose flavors based on what tastes good to you and you won't go wrong. To guide you further, a list of delicious flavor combinations for cakes, fillings, and icings follows.

**LEFT:** A chocolate buttercream extravaganza, iced to perfection and covered in sugar flowers and gold-leaf sugary stars, is perfect for a late-evening wedding under the stars. Created by Ron Ben-Israel Cakes.

**PAGE 43:** This petite Fabergé-inspired jewel-box cake conceals cheesecake inside. It is covered with Belgian white chocolate that has been colored royal blue, decorated with swirls of edible gold dust, and topped with a nosegay of white-chocolate roses and ribbon. Created by Susan Morgan of Elegant Cheese Cakes.

# CAKE, FILLING, AND ICING COMBINATIONS

CARROT CAKE with orange-scented cream-cheese filling and vanilla spice buttercream icing

CHOCOLATE-FUDGE CAKE filled with rich white-chocolate mousse and fresh raspberries, iced with a creamy white-chocolate buttercream

CLASSIC WHITE CAKE filled with fresh whipped cream and sliced strawberries, iced with an orange-scented buttercream

COFFEE SPONGE CAKE with rum-laced custard, covered in marzipan with mocha-mousse filling and rich, rolled-chocolate icing

CREAMY CHEESECAKE with a coffee-scented buttercream icing, and a white-chocolate fondant covering

LEMON CAKE with an airy lemon-mousse filling, fresh raspberries, and a lemon-scented buttercream icing

LEMON POUND CAKE filled with smooth lemon curd and fresh blueberries, finished with fresh whipped cream

MOIST HAZELNUT GÉNOISE, washed with cognac, layered with white- and dark-chocolate ganache, iced with an espresso buttercream

ORANGE-BLOSSOM YELLOW CAKE filled with raspberry mousse and fresh raspberries, finished with pale pink pistachio-scented buttercream icing

PUMPKIN SPICE CAKE with cream-cheese filling, crystallized ginger, walnuts, and dried cranberries, iced with a ginger-scented buttercream

SOUR-CREAM FUDGE CAKE with toasted hazelnut slices, smooth milk-chocolate ganache filling, iced with coffee liqueur buttercream

WHITE-CHOCOLATE SPONGE CAKE filled with rich chocolate mousse, studded with fresh raspberries, iced with creamy raspberry-flavored (or framboise) buttercream

If you are serving a cake with nuts in it, be sure to have the cake server notify guests (in case of food allergies).

## CHEESECAKES

Many couples are opting for cheesecake in place of the traditional flour-and-sugar cake. If you and your fiancé want this kind of cake, you should contact a baker that specializes in cheesecakes. There are special considerations, including the heavy weight of the cake and its need for constant refrigeration. Cheesecakes can be iced with buttercream or covered with fondant or marzipan, just like a flour cake.

# DECOR
## ADORNMENTS

ATIONS

FINISHING
TOUCHES

4

Your finished cake may display any number or combination of decorating techniques and decorations. The icing or cake covering is the canvas for your decorations. The most common decorations used are cake toppers, dragées, and gum paste or marzipan flowers or fruit. Piping is also a common technique for adding finishing touches to the cake. Piping utilizes a pastry bag of icing and a variety of tips. A star tip makes a star-like decoration, while a round tip is great for dots or writing. You can decorate a cake using piping techniques only, although most of the time a decorator will ice a cake, pipe a border around the perimeter of the base and tiers, and then add other kinds of decoration.

OPPOSITE: (top left) Delicate crystallized violets and pansies, courtesy of Meadowsweets, maintain their original beauty; (bottom right) Seashells fashioned from gum paste by Ellen Bartlett of Cakes To Remember; Vintage wedding-cake toppers from the 1920s (top) and the 1940s (bottom), courtesy of Cathy Cook.

PAGE 49: (detail on page 6) This all-white classic could be the centerpiece at any wedding, in any setting, and in any season. The cake is covered in white fondant with crimped edges. Gum-paste roses and royal icing borders complete this beautiful confection. Designed by Doris Schecter and Amilcar Palacious of My Most Favorite Dessert Company.

PAGES 50-51: The soft look of this sweet cake (left) is achieved by covering fresh buttercream with patterned fondant. A special rolling pin is used to roll out the fondant, creating translucent windows for the blue petal dust to shine through. Gum-paste bows and a dainty bouquet complete the look. Created by Ellen Baumwoll of Bijoux Doux Specialty Cakes. This all-white fondant cake (right) is adorned exclusively with silver dragées and a loose cornelli pattern, creating a very simple, yet sophisticated presentation. Created by Ellen Bartlett of Cakes To Remember.

# DECORATIONS

CAKE TOPPERS are no longer de rigueur on top of the cake. However, if you choose to have a cake top, you could use a vintage bride and groom, sculpted caricatures of the couple, or a crystal or porcelain replica of a symbol of love, such as doves or hearts. A bouquet of fresh or sugared flowers, ribbons or bows, or monograms made from sugar are also options.

DRAGÉES, shiny, edible silver or gold balls that come in varying sizes, can be used to dress up any kind of cake.

GUM PASTE, sometimes called sugar dough, is made from a base of sugar and gelatin, is an extremely versatile molding material, and is completely edible. Most contemporary wedding cake decorations are made of gum paste. It can be colored and molded into realistic flowers, figures, fruits, bows, ribbons, seashells, and even cake toppers. These decorations hold up extremely well for extended periods of time.

MARZIPAN OR ALMOND PASTE, another edible molding material, is employed in much the same way as gum paste. Fruit decorations are often composed of marzipan, which has a distinct almond flavor.

SUGARED FRUITS & CRYSTALLIZED FLOWERS: Small fruits such as grapes, kumquats, and strawberries can be coated with sugar to give them a soft, dewey look. Crystallized flowers are preserved with sugar so that they retain their original color and beauty.

# PIPING TECHNIQUES

BASKETWEAVE: A technique that features interwoven vertical and horizontal lines to create the effect of a basket.

BORDERING: A decorative edging piped around the perimeter of your cake and cake tiers.

CORNELLI: An elaborate and beautiful technique of piping that yields a lacelike effect.

DOTS OR DOTTED SWISS: A pattern of tiny pearl-like dots piped on the iced cake to resemble dotted Swiss fabric.

FLOWERS: Certain kinds of flowers can be created using a pastry bag and tips, such as roses, lilacs, and lilies of the valley. Piped flowers tend to have a heavier look than sugar or gum-paste flowers.

LACE POINTS: Royal icing is used to create delicate lace patterns that are then attached to the cake.

VINES & LEAVES: Authentic-looking green vines and leaves can be piped on the cake as a backdrop to iced, real, or sugar flowers.

WEDDING CAKES AND FLOWERS go hand in hand. Fresh flowers are sometimes used to decorate the cake, but be cautious: Many flowers are poisonous and should not be used. Flowers from the florist are routinely sprayed with insecticide, and if they are placed on your cake, you and your guests will be exposed to those poisons. I recommend using fresh, seasonal flowers from organic growers or from your own backyard. Also, use only nonpoisonous flowers; some of the most beautiful and delicate flowers, such as lilies of the valley and irises, are highly toxic to humans. If you don't have a nearby organic grower or flowers of your own, you can buy organic edible flowers or crystallized flowers from several growers who ship. Whether you decide to use fresh or gumpaste flowers, make arrangements with your caterer to insure that all inedible decorations are removed from the cake before it is served.

OPPOSITE: A lively bouquet of anemones, dill, and fritalleria, designed by Rebecca Cole of Cole Creates for a country wedding.

COMMONLY USED EDIBLE FLOWERS

# Borage
# Calendula
# Chrysanthemums
# Day Lilies
# English Daisies
# Fuschia
# Johnny Jump-ups
# Lavender

Lilacs
Nasturtiums
Pansies
Petunias
Roses
Snapdragons
Sunflowers
Violets

FRESH FRUIT is another nice option in addition to (or in lieu of) flowers. An off-white cake with clusters of sugared red raspberries and fresh mint leaves, or pure-white tiers covered in dewy fresh strawberries makes a very simple and beautiful statement. Kumquats, plain or dipped in sugar, look beautiful on a pale yellow cake. Champagne grapes are delicate and elegant draped against a soft pink- or pale-green-tinted background. Figs can be used whole or cut in half to dress a fall cake. In addition, fruits can be replicated in miniature in marzipan. They are beautiful to look at if created by a skilled artisan and delicious to eat, too.

OPPOSITE: This charming cake is decorated with miniature marzipan fruit and autumn leaves. Change the fruits to suit the season. Created by Rosemary Littman of Rosemary's Cakes.

BAK

CHOOSING·A·WEDDING·CAKE

KER

5

Choosing your wedding-cake baker is one of the more fun details of planning for your big day. Shop around: Word-of-mouth, the yellow pages, and the Internet are all good resources. Regional bridal publications are also helpful, as are florists and bridal consultants. If you search the web, you will find that many bakers are

posting photographs or "cake galleries," so that you can view their work and get a sense of the kinds of cakes that they specialize in. Be aware that some of these sites post photographs of other bakers' cakes. It is very common for bakers to copy each other's work, so often you will see knock-offs of cakes that have appeared in magazines or books. Make sure that the cake you see on a baker's website is the creation of that baker.

When you have made an appointment with a baker, bring with you anything that will give the baker clues about what you might like to incorporate into your cake. Fabric swatches of your dress or bridesmaids' dresses, magazine photographs of cakes, a vintage cake topper you plan to use—all of these things will help give shape to the perfect cake design for you.

Ordinarily, a large wedding cake will sit on top of a nondescript cake board because the cake is too large to fit on an attractive platter. Have your baker dress up the cake board by piping a design directly onto the board around the cake or covering the board in fondant. Or, if you prefer a smaller cake, search for a beautiful antique cake plate, a gorgeous silver platter, or a painted ceramic or glass plate.

Determine your cake budget with the baker of your choice. Often people are surprised at the cost of the wedding cake, but remind yourself that the wedding cake is an important element of your wedding reception and that it should be treated as such. The cost of a wedding cake can vary drastically from region to region, and there are many other factors that will help determine the cost of your cake. If your cake is elaborate, with an abundance of handmade sugar decorations or flowers and intricate piping work, naturally it will be more expensive than a modest, simply styled cake. And as a rule, fondant is more expensive than buttercream.

A wedding cake for fifty to one hundred guests can take your baker and his or her staff as little as three days to more than a week to bake and decorate, depending on the style of

your cake. Labor is probably the most expensive element of your wedding cake. You are serving your wedding guests a fabulous dessert and a memorable work of art. Some bakers charge by the design of the cake, and some charge by the slice. You may pay anywhere from $2.50 to $20 per slice. Somewhere in the middle is a reasonable expectation. Be prepared to pay for delivery, too, which is usually an extra charge. Most bakers will ask for a deposit of 20 to 50 percent when you confirm with them, and the balance several weeks before your wedding day.

If the cost of the cake you desire is truly prohibitive, you have some options, if your baker is willing to cooperate. Sometimes a baker will agree to do a smaller version of the cake you want; this is the cake you will display and later cut. Instead of serving all of your guests from this cake, however, you can have a less expensive sheet cake to serve the remainder of the guests. You can also serve guests smaller slices of cake, and add ice cream or fresh fruit. Occasionally, you may find a baker who is willing to create a "dummy" cake for display only, but most bakers are unwilling to do this. If you have a display-only cake, you will serve your guests a sheet cake from the kitchen.

Check with your banquet hall or caterer to find out if they will charge you a "cutting fee." An extra fee of up to $3 per person may be charged if an outside baker provides the cake. Check to see if a cutting fee is itemized in your contract, and know that it is often negotiable. You are paying for waitstaff for a certain number of hours, and serving the cake will be part of their service already, so try to negotiate your way out of this extra charge if it's in your catering contract.

**PAGES 62-63:** (left, detail, full view on page 80) Royal icing has been used to pipe the borders and the fine details on this extraordinary cake by François Payard of Payard Patisserie. This miniature wedding cake (right) is finished in a pale yellow fondant and decorated with royal icing. A fondant ribbon tops it off. Created by Scrumptions.

**ABOVE:** (detail, full view on page 109) The edible flowers from this multitiered cake will be removed at cutting time and used as a garnish on each guest's dessert plate. Created by Ron Ben-Israel Cakes.

# A WEDDING-CAKE CHECKLIST

SET UP AN APPOINTMENT with at least three bakers once you know the details of your wedding day. The sooner you do this, the better off you will be, as many bakers book up to a year in advance. It's also a good idea to shop around so that you have an understanding of the range of prices and the different styles bakers bring to their cakes.

DISCUSS time, place, room, season, flowers, and dress. This information will give the wedding-cake designer a sense of you and your wedding style, and all of these details are important to creating your unique cake.

LOOK AT PHOTOGRAPHS. Your baker should have photographs of other cakes he or she has done. Be sure to ask if the photographs represent work done by their current staff.

ASK HOW FAR IN ADVANCE your cake will be baked. Sometimes bakers prepare the cake and freeze it, but this is not recommended. It's your wedding, so insist on a fresh cake. If your cake is very large and elaborately decorated, however, it may require baking a week or more in advance.

SET UP A TASTING APPOINTMENT. If your baker doesn't have samples on hand, ask to set a date for a tasting so you can sample different cakes and fillings.

KEEP AN OPEN MIND. If you have specific ideas, share them with your baker, but keep in mind the possibilities and remember that this is a collaboration between you, your fiancé, and the cake designer. You may wind up with a cake that exceeds your wildest dreams.

TALK LOGISTICS. Ask about delivery. Find out if your cake delivery is via a refrigerated truck, and whether your bakery does their own delivery or hires an outside delivery service. If they rely on an outside service, be sure that they have experience delivering wedding cakes (think about how difficult it is to transport food in your car, then consider the dimensions of a wedding cake!). Ask whether or not your cake will be assembled at the reception, who will do it, and how far in advance of the guests arriving it will be done. Get a specific time the cake will be delivered to the reception site. Ask if it will require refrigeration once there, and be sure that the baker has the name and number of a contact person (your catering manager or your wedding planner) in case the cake needs special attention.

GET EVERYTHING IN WRITING. Once you have narrowed the possibilities and have chosen a design you are excited about, get the date, the sketch, the dimensions, the details of delivery, and the total price including delivery on paper.

EXPECT TO LEAVE A DEPOSIT. Most bakers will want some money up front, usually 20 to 50 percent, with the remainder due several weeks before the wedding day.

# REC
## FOR BAKING
### YOUR OWN CAKE

IPES

6

If you, or a friend or family member, decide to bake your wedding cake instead of hiring a professional to do it, there are a few things you need to know to achieve optimum results. Making a wedding cake is, of course, a little more involved than baking an ordinary cake, and whether you're making your own or have chosen to

create a cake for someone you love, you'll want perfection. Read this chapter thoroughly. If you follow the directions carefully and pay close attention to tips and techniques, your cake will be a success.

To anybody who wants to bake his or her own wedding cake, I strongly suggest that you buy a copy of Rose Levy Beranbaum's classic reference, *The Cake Bible*. Her recipes are foolproof and her insight is invaluable when undertaking such an important cake. With Rose's permission, I've included two of these marvelous cake recipes in this chapter—one for yellow or white cake, the other for chocolate. These delicious and dependable recipes are also the basis of the three do-it-yourself cake designs that close this chapter.

The number of guests attending your wedding reception will determine the size of the cake that you bake. Wedding cake portions are traditionally quite small due to their richness. The yields for the cake recipes in this chapter are based on servings just 2-inches deep by 4-inches high, and ¾-inch wide. Two of the cake designs featured in this chapter have three tiers (12, 9, and 6 inches across, respectively), but one has square tiers, the other round. Each is large enough to serve 150 people. The third cake is round and has a 12-inch base and a 9-inch top, and will serve 100 to 125 guests.

CAKE BASICS: ASSEMBLY AND DECORATION
CREATING THE LAYERS

Slicing the cake layers into level tiers can be difficult, but by following the directions below and working carefully, you should get good results. Don't worry too much if your cake slices are uneven; after you fill the layers, you will rebuild them, replacing the slices in the same way you took them off. You also can use the filling and icing to add a bit of height to an uneven cake, and to help hide any mistakes you have made.

Once your cakes have been baked and completely cooled,

chill them for several hours. This will result in a firmer cake and fewer crumbs when slicing. Next, trim off the bulging top of each cake to create a level surface. To make this job easier, use a turntable or a lazy Susan and a 12-inch serrated knife.

Assuming you are making a three-tiered cake, you should now have six level cakes in three different sizes. Take one of the cakes, and mark its side at $1/2$-inch intervals, starting at the bottom and working toward the top. You will end up with two or maybe three marks, depending on the height of your cake; when sliced this will create three or four thin layers.

To make the layers, set the cake on your turntable and place the edge of your serrated knife against the uppermost mark on the cake. Holding your knife hand steady, apply pressure to the knife while turning the turntable; this will make a straight and level slice all the way through the cake. Lift an edge of the new layer and carefully slide a cake cardboard cut to the same size underneath it; set aside.

Repeat this process until you have three or maybe four layers. Using a pastry brush, moisten each of the layers with syrup (see page 80 for a basic syrup recipe)—about $1/4$ cup of syrup for each of smaller layers, and up to 1 cup on larger cake layers. The syrup will impart any flavor you give it and will keep the layers moist.

Repeat this process with the other five cakes until all of the layers have been sliced, placed on cake cardboards, and brushed with syrup.

### FILLING THE LAYERS

The next step is filling the layers. To help keep your cakes level, reassemble the layers in the same order that you sliced and removed them.

Starting with what will be the bottom layer of your largest or base cake, pipe or spoon your filling on top of the cake layer (see page 81 for a lemon cream filling recipe). A pastry bag with a No. 789 icing tip can be used to do this; just fill the bag with the filling. Then, starting at the outside edge of the cake, pipe a large spiral (or square if the cake is square) on top of the cake. Using a long icing spatula, smooth the filling over the top of the layer. There should be $1/2$ to $3/4$ of an inch of filling on top of each layer. To help maintain the cake's height, chill each layer for 10 minutes before placing the next cake layer on top.

Slide the next layer of cake off its cardboard and place it on top of the first layer of filling. Pipe or spoon filling on top of the cake, again smoothing the filling with a long icing spatula. Repeat with the remaining equal-sized layers, chilling between applications. If any filling oozes out between the layers, use a clean icing spatula to remove it and smooth the edges. The filling should be even with the edges of the cake, not bulging out between the layers; excess filling could cause problems when it's time to ice the cake.

After all the layers have been filled and assembled (the tops of the cakes do not need any filling, of course), refrigerate the cakes for at least 30 minutes, until the filling is firm.

### CRUMB COATING THE CAKE

After the filled cakes have been chilled, it is time to crumb coat them. A crumb coating is a thin layer of icing that is used to seal the cake. It is the cake's very first layer of icing, which fills in any holes or gaps and seals in the crumbs in preparation for the final icing, or a covering of fondant or marzipan.

As with the filling, the icing can be applied to the cake using either an icing spatula or a pastry bag with a No. 789 icing tip. Ice each of the cakes as smoothly as possible, keeping the edges of the cakes square and the tops and sides smooth and even. The crumb coating should cover the cakes and fill any holes with a thin layer of icing, but you should still be able to see the cakes underneath. Once the cakes have been crumb coated, they can be refrigerated for several days.

### SUPPORTING AND TIERING THE CAKE

The recipes and designs in this chapter are for two- or three-tiered wedding cakes. Each tier will be approximately 6 to 8 inches high once the cake is filled and iced, but it's not unheard of for wedding cakes to boast 10-inch tiers.

The bottom and middle cakes of three- or more-tiered cakes always require special supports so that they don't collapse and sink into one another. These supports can be created from ⅛-inch wooden dowels, plastic drinking straws, or wooden skewers cut to the exact height of your cake.

For example, when working with a 12-inch round or square cake that will be topped by a 9-inch cake, start by inserting a 12-inch length of dowel, straw, or skewer into the center of the base cake, making sure that you thrust it all the way through the cake so that the other end touches the cake board. Cut the length of dowel that is sticking out of the top of cake so that it is level with the top of the cake. Remove the dowel and use this as your guide to cut three more supports exactly the same length. Next, center a 9-inch cake pan over the 12-inch cake and gently press down to make a slight impression in your icing. Insert the four dowels all the way into the cake, positioning them one-inch inside the impression at 12:00, 3:00, 6:00, and 9:00, respectively. These supports should be level with the top of the cake. Repeat this process for any cake that supports additional cakes on top. The supports should remain inside the cake until serving time, when the cake will be disassembled and the supports removed.

If the cake design calls for separated tiers, you can buy cake pillars or separators. The pillars, which are made of plastic, come in lengths of 3, 5, 7, 9, or 12 inches and help support and separate the tiers of your cake. Separators and pillars are typically covered with icing or decorations so that they blend in visually with the rest of the cake. They will be removed when the cake is disassembled at serving time.

There are two different methods with which to utilize the pillars. Either method will work to support the cakes, but if the base cake is higher than 12 inches, you'll need to use the first method, as you won't be able to purchase pillars tall enough to maintain space between the two tiers.

The first method follows the standard instruction for stacking cakes; insert four supporting dowels or skewers directly into the base cake. Next, attach separator plates to both ends of the four pillars (whichever length you choose). Center the stand on top of the base cake and its internal supports. You're now ready to place the second cake on top of its plate.

The second method does away with the bottom plate and instead of inserting the traditional dowels, you put the pillars of the stand directly into the cake. In purchasing pillars for this method, it is important to consider the height of your finished base cake and the amount of space you want between the two cakes. For example, if you want a 3-inch separation between the tiers and each cake is 4 inches high, you will need at least a 7-inch pillar sunk 4 inches into the bottom tier for adequate support.

Any dowel, skewer, or straw supports should be inserted into the cakes after the final icing, except when the cake is covered in fondant, when the supports should be added after the crumb coating. Wooden dowels, skewers, pillars, plates, and separators can all be ordered from the cake and baking supply houses listed in the resource guide.

ICING THE CAKE

Buttercream is a very popular choice for icing wedding cakes because it is delicious, takes color beautifully, and can be used for a variety of piping techniques. Buttercream can be refrigerated, but if your cake will be displayed for long periods during hot weather, solid vegetable shortening should be added to the icing. This helps keep buttercream from melting, but it does detract from its flavor.

Icing a cake to a smooth, flat finish takes a great deal of patience and a lot of practice. An icing spatula, a small offset spatula, and an icing blade are the tools you will need to create a smooth surface and sharp, clean edges.

Liquid or paste coloring can be added to buttercream (see page 82 for an excellent Swiss buttercream recipe) and blended in a standing mixer. Be sure to add only a toothpick drop of coloring at a time, however, until you get the desired color.

Ice your cakes only after each tier has been crumb coated and chilled for several hours. If your buttercream is too cold, it will be difficult to spread; too warm and it may slide off your cakes. To warm buttercream, leave it at room temperature until it is easy to spread, give it a quick spin in the mixer to speed the process. If the buttercream is too warm, chilling it for approximately 15 minutes will correct its consistency.

Apply the icing to your cakes using a pastry bag and a No. 789 icing tip. Alternatively, spoon the icing onto the cake and use an icing blade to move and smooth the icing over the top and sides of the cake. Whichever method you choose, only apply enough icing to cover the cake completely. Buttercream is rich, and too much of it is unappetizing.

Each cake should be iced to perfection and well chilled before assembling the tiers. After the icing has been applied, the cakes can be individually boxed and refrigerated for up to 3 days.

## DECORATING WITH FONDANT

Rolled fondant is made primarily from sugar, solid vegetable shortening, and glycerine, and on its own probably wouldn't taste very good. However, as part of a layered and filled cake it tastes quite nice and makes a beautiful cake covering. I don't encourage making fondant at home, because most home bakers lack a mixer large and powerful enough to make it. Instead, I have listed several sources for cake decorations and baking supplies (see page 111) that all carry fondant.

Fondant is usually sold in 2- to 8-pound packages. You will need about 8 pounds of fondant to cover the three-tiered cakes described in this chapter. A 12-inch cake takes $3\frac{1}{2}$ pounds of fondant, a 9-inch cake takes $2\frac{1}{2}$ pounds, and a 6-inch cake requires $1\frac{1}{2}$ pounds.

Fondant can be colored using food paste coloring, also available at cake decorating supply houses. Do not use liquid food color as it may change the consistency of the fondant. To add the coloring, cut off a chunk of fondant, then knead a dab of the paste coloring into the fondant, adding more coloring and fondant as necessary, until you are satisfied with the results. It is imperative that you color enough fondant to cover the entire cake, because it is very difficult to match colors if you do separate batches for each tier.

To help the fondant adhere to the cake, first ice the cakes with a crumb coating and refrigerate. When you are ready to roll the fondant, lightly spray a clean, smooth, parchment-covered surface with nonstick vegetable spray. Using a rolling pin and enough fondant to cover the base cake, roll the fondant into a disk about $\frac{1}{4}$-inch thick.

Transfer the fondant to the iced cake by wrapping it gently around a rolling pin, then position the rolling pin over the cake so that one side of the fondant touches the side of the cake plate. Slowly move the pin across the cake, unrolling the fondant. Smooth the covering over the top and sides of the cake with your hands or a smoothing tool, removing any air pockets or bumps and directing excess fondant down and away from the bottom of the cake.

Work quickly to avoid too much handling of the fondant. You should first cover the bottom-tier cake with fondant, then trim around the edge, level with the cake board. Next cover the middle and top tiers with fondant, taking the fondant over and under the cardboard edges and trimming off any excess. Then let each of the cakes rest for several hours or overnight to firm-up before decorating.

Once the cakes have been covered in fondant, they will stay fresh at room temperature for 2 to 3 days. Refrigerating fondant is risky because the moisture from refrigeration can cause condensation, which will cause colors to bleed and break down your fondant. Although it is not recommended, some people do refrigerate fondant cakes. If you must follow suit, box the cakes and individually cover the boxes with a double layer of plastic wrap. When you are ready to finish decorating your cake, first uncover the tiers and let them come to room temperature.

## PLANNING AHEAD

TIME Plan to spend 4 days to a week preparing, baking, and decorating your wedding cake. This of course excludes time spent planning a design and ordering the necessary equipment and special ingredients you will need to complete even a simple cake.

EXPENSE It will cost at least several hundred dollars to make a simple cake for 150 people. Unless you have the proper equipment and tools already, be prepared to spend most of that sum on equipment.

SIZE Most home refrigerators are too small to accommodate a cake for 50 to 150 people. If you have friends in the restaurant or bakery business, they may be willing to loan you space in their walk-in refrigerators. The tiers must be individually boxed, and the boxes should be 4 to 6 inches larger than the base of the cakes.

DELIVERY When it is time to deliver your cake, you will need a large, strong cardboard box, some non-skid material to go underneath the box, and a vehicle that's large and cool enough to transport the cake. If the weather is warm, make sure you have air conditioning so your cake doesn't melt. Give yourself plenty of time to transport the cake—you'll want to drive with extra caution to avoid sudden stops and starts.

EMERGENCY KIT Even with careful planning and handling, a thumb may still get stuck in the icing or a flower may fall off the cake. Professional bakers always carry pastry bags, couplings and tips, icing, spatulas, and extra flowers or decorations to handle any minor repairs that may come up in transporting the cake.

## CAKE TIPS

1. Make sure your oven temperature is true!

2. Always sift the flour, baking powder, and baking soda into the measuring vessel.

3. Always use sweet, unsalted butter.

4. Butter should always be at room temperature. Slicing cold butter will speed the warming process.

5. Add nuts and fruits to the batter last, mixing them in with a wooden spoon.

6. Always butter and flour the cake pans.

7. Always fill cake pans 3/4 full.

8. Cool cakes in their pans for 15 minutes before turning them out onto baking racks.

9. Chill the cakes before trimming, filling, and icing.

10. Crumb coat cakes before covering and icing.

11. Chill the cake after each filling, crumb coating, and icing (only if you are using buttercream—do not refrigerate fondant!).

12. To avoid sliding cake tiers, always secure cakes that sit directly on top of one another with a dollop of royal icing or buttercream.

13. Secure the base cake cardboard to the cake base with double-sided adhesive tape.

# RECIPES

Three-Tier White or Yellow Butter Wedding Cake

Three-Tier Chocolate Butter Wedding Cake

Simple Syrup

Lemon Cream Filling

Swiss Meringue Buttercream

Chocolate Ganache Icing

Royal Icing

Three-Tier Square Cake with Fresh Flowers

Pale Pink Fondant Cake with Crystallized Flowers

White Fondant Cake with Fresh Fruit Decoration

ROSE LEVY BERANBAUM is a master baker and a superstar in the world of desserts. The two marvelous wedding cake recipes that follow are from her award-winning *The Cake Bible* (pages 484 and 486), published by William Morrow in 1988 and followed by her equally foolproof *The Pie and Pastry Bible* (Scribner, 1999). In addition to these two basic wedding cake recipes, *The Cake Bible* offers many recipes for wonderful fillings and icings that are perfect for wedding cakes, plus helpful rules and tips for bakers.

You will need a 5-quart mixer for both of Rose's cake recipes.

## ROSE LEVY BERANBAUM'S
## THREE-TIER WHITE OR YELLOW BUTTER WEDDING CAKE
### SERVES 150

| For two 6-inch by 2-inch layers and two 9-inch by 2-inch layers | | | |
|---|---|---|---|
| INGREDIENTS | MEASURE | WEIGHT | |
| ROOM TEMPERATURE | VOLUME | POUNDS/OUNCES | KILOGRAMS/GRAMS |
| 9 large egg whites *or* | 1 liquid cup + 2 tablespoons* | 9.5 ounces | 270 grams |
| 12 large egg yolks | 7 fluid ounces* | 7.75 ounces | 223 grams |
| milk | 2 cups* | 17 ounces | 484 grams |
| vanilla | 1 tablespoon + 1½ teaspoons | | 18 grams |
| sifted cake flour | 6 cups | 1 pound 5 ounces | 600 grams |
| sugar | 3 cups | 1 pound 5 ounces | 600 grams |
| baking powder | 2 tablespoons + 2 teaspoons | | 39 grams |
| salt | 1½ teaspoons | | 10 grams |
| unsalted butter (must be softened) | 1½ cups | 12 ounces | 340 grams |
| For two 12-inch by 2-inch layers | | | |
| INGREDIENTS | MEASURE | WEIGHT | |
| ROOM TEMPERATURE | VOLUME | POUNDS/OUNCES | KILOGRAMS/GRAMS |
| 10½ large egg whites *or* | 1⅓ liquid cups* | 11 ounces | 315 grams |
| 14 large egg yolks | 1 liquid cup* | 9 ounces | 260 grams |
| milk | 2⅓ liquid cups* | 1 pound 3.75 ounces | 564 grams |
| vanilla | 1 tablespoon + 2¼ teaspoons | | 21 grams |
| sifted cake flour | 7 cups | 1 pound 8.5 ounces | 700 grams |
| sugar | 3½ cups | 1 pound 8.5 ounces | 700 grams |
| baking powder | 2 tablespoons + 1¾ teaspoons | | 38 grams |
| salt | 1¾ teaspoons | | 12 grams |
| unsalted butter (must be softened) | 1¾ cups | 14 ounces | 400 grams |

*Use a glass measuring cup.

1. Grease the pans, line the bottoms with parchment or wax paper, and then grease again and flour. Arrange 2 oven racks as close to the center of the oven as possible with at least 3 inches between them. Preheat the oven to 350° F.

2. In a medium bowl, lightly combine the whites or yolks, ¼ of the milk, and the vanilla.

3. In a large mixing bowl combine all the dry ingredients and mix on low speed for 1 minute to blend. Add the butter and remaining milk. Mix on low speed until the dry ingredients are moistened. Beat at medium speed (high speed if using a hand mixer) for 1½ minutes to aerate and develop the cake's structure. Scrape down the sides.

4. Gradually beat in the egg mixture in 3 batches, beating for 20 seconds after each addition to incorporate the ingredients and strengthen the structure. Scrape down the sides.

5. Scrape the batter into the prepared pans, filling about halfway, and smooth with a spatula. Arrange the pans in the oven so that air can circulate around them. Do not allow them to touch each other or the oven walls. Bake 25 to 35 minutes for 6-inch layers, 35 to 45 minutes for 9-inch layers, and 40 to 50 minutes for 12-inch layers or until a tester inserted near the center comes out clean and the cake springs back when pressed lightly in the center. In the 6-inch and 9-inch pans, the cakes should start to shrink from the sides only after removal from the oven. The 12-inch layers should bake until they just start to shrink from the sides. To promote more even baking, turn the 12-inch layers 180° (halfway around) halfway through the baking time. Do this quickly so the oven temperature does not drop.

6. Allow the cakes to cool in the pans on racks for 10 minutes (20 minutes for 12-inch layers). Loosen the sides with a spatula and invert onto greased wire racks. To prevent splitting, reinvert and cool completely before wrapping airtight with plastic wrap and foil.

NOTE: Do not underbake the 12-inch layers. When preparing the cake more than 24 hours ahead of serving or if extra moistness is desired, Rose recommends sprinkling layers with 3 cups of syrup (see page 80 for a Simple Syrup recipe).

FINISHED HEIGHT: Each layer is about 1½ inches.

STORE: Airtight: 2 days room temperature, 5 days refrigerated, 2 months frozen.

SERVE: At room temperature.

**ROSE LEVY BERANBAUM'S**
## THREE-TIER CHOCOLATE BUTTER WEDDING CAKE
### SERVES 150

| For two 6-inch by 2-inch layers and two 9-inch by 2-inch layers | | | |
|---|---|---|---|
| **INGREDIENTS** | **MEASURE** | **WEIGHT** | |
| ROOM TEMPERATURE | VOLUME | POUNDS/OUNCES | KILOGRAMS/GRAMS |
| 6 large eggs | 10 scant fluid ounces* | 10.5 ounces (weighed without shells) | 300 grams (weighed without shells) |
| water (boiling) | 2 liquid cups* | 1 pound 0.75 ounce | 473 grams |
| vanilla | 1 tablespoon + 1½ teaspoons | | 18 grams |
| sifted cake flour | 4¾ cups | 1 pound 0.5 ounce | 475 grams |
| unsweetened cocoa (Dutch-processed) | 1¼ cups + 2 tablespoons (lightly spooned into cup) | 4.5 ounces | 125 grams |
| sugar | 3 cups | 1 pound 5 ounces | 600 grams |
| baking powder | 3 tablespoons | 1.5 ounces | 44 grams |
| salt | 1½ teaspoons | | 10 grams |
| unsalted butter | 2 cups | 16 ounces | 454 grams |
| For two 12-inch by 2-inch layers | | | |
| **INGREDIENTS** | **MEASURE** | **WEIGHT** | |
| ROOM TEMPERATURE | VOLUME | POUNDS/OUNCES | KILOGRAMS/GRAMS |
| 7 large eggs | 11 fluid ounces* | 12.25 ounces (weighed without shells) | 350 grams (weighed without shells) |
| water (boiling) | 2 ⅓ liquid cups* | 1 pound 3.5 ounces | 550 grams |
| vanilla | 1 tablespoon + 2¼ teaspoons | | 21 grams |
| sifted cake flour | 5½ cups | 1 pound 3.5 ounces | 553 grams |
| unsweetened cocoa (Dutch-processed) | 1½ cups + 2 tablespoons (lightly spooned into cup) | 5 ounces | 147 grams |
| sugar | 3½ cups | 1 pound 8.5 ounces | 700 grams |
| baking powder | 2 tablespoons + 2¾ teaspoons | | 43 grams |
| salt | 1¾ teaspoons | | 12 grams |
| unsalted butter | 2⅓ cups | 18.5 ounces | 525 grams |

*Use a glass measuring cup.

1. Grease the pans, line the bottoms with parchment or wax paper, and then grease again and flour. Arrange 2 oven racks as close to the center of the oven as possible with at least 3 inches between them. Preheat the oven to 350° F.

2. In a medium bowl whisk together the cocoa and boiling water until smooth and cool to room temperature.

3. In another medium bowl lightly combine the eggs, $\frac{1}{4}$ of the cocoa mixture, and the vanilla.

4. In a large mixing bowl combine all the remaining dry ingredients and mix on low speed for 1 minute to blend. Add the butter and remaining cocoa mixture. Mix on low speed until the dry ingredients are moistened. Beat at medium speed (high speed if using a hand mixer) for $1\frac{1}{2}$ minutes to aerate and develop the cake's structure. Scrape down the sides.

5. Gradually beat in the egg mixture in 3 batches, beating for 20 seconds after each addition to incorporate the ingredients and strengthen the structure. Scrape down the sides.

6. Scrape the batter into the prepared pans, filling about halfway, and smooth with a spatula. Arrange the pans in the oven so that air can circulate around them. Do not allow them to touch each other or the oven walls. Bake 25 to 35 minutes for 6-inch layers, 35 to 45 minutes for 9-inch layers, 40 to 50 minutes for 12-inch layers or until a tester inserted near the center comes out clean and the cake springs back when pressed lightly in the center. In the 6-inch and 9-inch pans, the cakes should start to shrink from the sides only after removal from the oven. The 12-inch layers should bake until they just start to shrink from the sides. To promote more even baking, turn the 12-inch layers 180° (halfway around) halfway through the baking time. Do this quickly so the oven temperature does not drop.

7. Allow the cakes to cool in the pans on racks for 10 minutes (20 minutes for 12-inch layers). Loosen the sides with a small metal spatula and invert onto greased wire racks. To prevent splitting, reinvert and cool completely before wrapping airtight with plastic wrap and heavy-duty foil.

NOTE: Do not underbake the 12-inch layers. If you cut the tops of the cake layers to make them more level, you will notice many small holes. Do not be alarmed because they will not show up when cake is sliced. The crumb will be fine and even. When preparing the cake more than 24 hours ahead of serving or if extra moistness is desired, Rose recommends sprinkling layers with 3 cups of syrup (see page 80 for a Simple Syrup recipe).

FINISHED HEIGHT: Each layer is about 1½ inches.

STORE: Airtight: 2 days room temperature, 5 days refrigerated, 2 months frozen.

SERVE: At room temperature.

## SIMPLE SYRUP
### MAKES 3 CUPS

This is a basic recipe for sugar syrup to be brushed on all of the cake layers before they are stacked. The syrup keeps the layers moist and the liqueur adds a subtle flavor. One half cup extract can be substituted for the liqueur if you prefer.

| INGREDIENTS | MEASURE | WEIGHT | |
|---|---|---|---|
| ROOM TEMPERATURE | VOLUME | POUNDS/OUNCES | KILOGRAMS/GRAMS |
| sugar | one cup | 7 ounces | 200 grams |
| water | 2 ½ liquid cups* | 21 ounces | 590 grams |
| optional liqueur *or* extract† | ½ liquid cup* | 4 ounces | 120 grams |

*Use a glass measuring cup.

1. In a small saucepan combine the sugar and water and bring to a boil, stirring constantly. As soon as the sugar has dissolved, remove the pan from the heat, cover, and let cool.

2. When the liquid is completely cool, stir in the liqueur or extract of your choice.

**NOTE:** Simple Syrup can be stored for up to 1 month refrigerated in an airtight container.

**†SOME LIQUEUR OR EXTRACT OPTIONS ARE:** framboise, amaretto, Kahlúa, or Cointreau; or lemon, almond, coconut, or vanilla extract.

**LEFT:** A refined masterpiece of tiered squares (detail on page 62) covered in pale yellow buttercream and adorned with calla lilies, royal icing borders, and gold dragées by François Payard of Payard Patisserie.

# KAYE HANSEN'S
## LEMON CREAM FILLING
### MAKES 10 TO 12 CUPS

This delicious recipe comes from Kaye Hansen and her daughter Liv, the talented duo behind the Riviera Bakehouse in Ardsley, New York, and coauthors of *The Whimsical Bakehouse*, published by Clarkson Potter. The lemon curd is prepared first, then whipped cream is folded in to create a delicious smooth, lemony filling. The tartness of the lemon filling pairs delightfully with raspberries and yellow cake. This recipe can be halved or doubled with excellent results.

| INGREDIENTS | MEASURE | WEIGHT | |
| --- | --- | --- | --- |
| ROOM TEMPERATURE | VOLUME | POUNDS/OUNCES | KILOGRAMS/GRAMS |
| For the lemon curd: | | | |
| lemon juice (freshly squeezed) | 1 liquid cup (about 8 lemons)* | 8.75 ounces | 250 grams |
| sugar | 1 cup | 7 ounces | 200 grams |
| unsalted butter (must be softened) | ¾ cup | 6 ounces | 170 grams |
| lemon zest | 2 tablespoons | | 12 grams |
| 8 large eggs | 1½ liquid cups* | 14 ounces | 400 grams |
| For the whipped cream: | | | |
| heavy cream | 5 liquid cups* | 2.5 pounds | 1.13 kilograms |
| confectioners' sugar | ½ cup | 2 ounces | 57 grams |

*Use a glass measuring cup.

1. Combine the lemon juice, sugar, butter, and zest in a small nonreactive saucepan and bring to a boil. Remove from heat.

2. In a medium bowl whisk the eggs, then slowly whisk in the hot lemon juice. Return the mixture to the saucepan or double boiler and whisk constantly over low heat until the mixture coats the back of a wooden spoon (about 5 minutes). Do not let the mixture boil.

3. Strain the mixture through a fine-mesh sieve and transfer the curd into a large storage container; discard solids. Place a layer of plastic wrap directly on top of the lemon curd, and refrigerate for 1 hour. The curd will continue to thicken as it cools. To chill quickly, whisk the lemon curd over a bowl of ice water.

4. When the lemon curd is cool, whip the cream and confectioners' sugar in a small bowl until stiff. Gently fold the whipped cream into the lemon curd.

NOTE: Lemon curd can be stored for up to 5 days refrigerated in an airtight container. Once whipped cream is added, use it immediately.

## TOBA GARRETT'S
### SWISS MERINGUE BUTTERCREAM
#### MAKES 2 ½ QUARTS

A master cake designer and sugar-craft artist, Toba M. Garrett has studied with world renowned pastry chefs from North America, England, France, South Africa, Australia, and New Zealand. She teaches all levels of classical cake decorating and cookie design at Peter Kump's New York Cooking School.

This is Toba's favorite buttercream icing recipe. You will need a standing mixer with a 5-quart bowl to prepare it. The recipe must be doubled to ice a three-tiered cake large enough to serve 150 guests, but make one recipe at a time to avoid having the buttercream spill out of the mixer.

| INGREDIENTS | MEASURE | WEIGHT | |
|---|---|---|---|
| ROOM TEMPERATURE | VOLUME | POUNDS/OUNCES | KILOGRAMS/GRAMS |
| 10 to 12 large egg whites | 1 ½ liquid cups* | 12.75 ounces | 360 grams |
| sugar | 3 cups | 1 pound 5 ounces | 600 grams |
| unsalted butter | 6 cups | 3 pounds | 1.36 kilograms |
| optional liqueur *or* | | up to 3 ounces | |
| optional extract † | 2 tablespoons | | |

*Use a glass measuring cup.

1. Place the egg whites and sugar in the top of a double boiler set over simmering water. Lightly whisk them together until the egg white mixture is hot to the touch and a candy thermometer reads 140° F.

2. Pour the hot mixture into a room temperature mixing bowl and whip on medium-high speed, until the meringue has doubled in volume and cooled slightly to the touch. Meanwhile, cut up the butter into 2-inch pieces; the butter should be slightly moist on the outside but cold on the inside.

3. Remove the whip and attach a paddle to the mixer. Add half of the butter (1 ½ pounds) to the meringue immediately and pulsate the mixer several times (turning the mixer on and off in a zig-zag rhythm) until the meringue has covered the butter completely. Add the rest of the butter and pulsate the mixer several more times, until all of the butter is covered with the meringue.

Slowly raise the speed of the mixer, starting with the lowest speed and raising it every ten seconds until you reach a medium-high speed. If the meringue starts to curdle, just continue beating until the mixture turns into a smooth icing. Stop the mixer occasionally and, with a rubber spatula, scrape the buttercream off the sides of the bowl to make sure all the butter is incorporated.

4. Lower the mixing speed and add your flavoring of choice, beating for 3 more minutes to incorporate it. The buttercream should be light and fluffy.

NOTE: Swiss Meringue Buttercream can be refrigerated in an airtight container for up to 1 week, and frozen for up to 3 months. Allow the buttercream to come to room temperature and rewhip in a standing mixer.

†SOME LIQUEUR OR EXTRACT OPTIONS ARE: kirsch, framboise, Cointreau, rum, or Kahlúa; or orange, lemon, or almond extract.

**ELLEN BAUMWOLL'S**

CHOCOLATE GANACHE ICING

MAKES 2 QUARTS

Ellen is the owner and creative talent behind Bijoux Doux Specialty Cakes, a small custom cake house in Manhattan.

This ganache is simple to make and intensely chocolate, and works as either an icing or a filling.

| INGREDIENTS | MEASURE | WEIGHT | |
|---|---|---|---|
| ROOM TEMPERATURE | VOLUME | POUNDS/OUNCES | KILOGRAMS/GRAMS |
| semi- or bittersweet chocolate | 3 pounds | | 1.36 kilograms |
| heavy cream | 3 ½ liquid cups* | 1 pound 12 ounces | 794 grams |

*Use a glass measuring cup.

1. Break the chocolate into 3-inch pieces and place a third of them in the bowl of a food processor. Pulse the chocolate in batches until it is all chopped into small pieces, a little smaller than chocolate chips. Move the chocolate to a large mixing bowl.

2. In a heavy saucepan heat the cream until it comes to a boil. Pour the cream over the chocolate and stir with a wooden spoon until all of the chocolate is melted and emulsified with the cream. The ganache should be smooth and glossy. Transfer it to a large storage container and place a layer of plastic wrap directly on top of it to avoid forming a skin. Cool to room temperature; as the ganache cools it will thicken.

3. When you are ready to use the ganache, stir with a rubber spatula to smooth and emulsify. Do not use an electric mixer.

NOTE: Chocolate Ganache Icing will keep for 3 days at room temperature or 2 weeks refrigerated in an airtight container. It can be frozen for up to 6 months. To soften chilled ganache, put it in the microwave for a few seconds. Stir it gently and use immediately.

# ROYAL ICING

## MAKES 2½ TO 3 CUPS

Royal icing is wonderful for fine detail on cakes. It air dries to a hard consistency, which makes it perfect for piping decorations or as glue to attach decorations to a cake. It keeps well in a sealed container at room temperature, but never refrigerate it as it does not stay firm in any kind of humidity. After storing royal icing for any length of time, stir well to restore its original consistency. The icing also can be left in a clean pastry bag overnight if necessary; place a damp cloth around the bag and seal in plastic wrap until ready to use. Royal icing will break down if it comes into contact with any kind of grease, so make sure all of your equipment and utensils are meticulously clean.

| INGREDIENTS | MEASURE | WEIGHT | |
|---|---|---|---|
| ROOM TEMPERATURE | VOLUME | POUNDS/OUNCES | KILOGRAMS/GRAMS |
| 4 large egg whites | ½ liquid cup* | 4.25 ounces | 120 grams |
| confectioners' sugar | 4 cups | 1 pound | 460 grams |
| cream of tartar | ½ teaspoon | | 1.55 grams |

*Use a glass measuring cup.

1. Place the egg whites in a glass bowl and stir briskly with a fork. Add ¼ cup of the confectioners' sugar and the cream of tartar, and stir until smooth. Continue adding the sugar, stirring constantly with the fork, until the icing is completely smooth.

NOTE: If you are not using Royal Icing immediately, place it in an airtight container and store at room temperature for up to 3 days.

OPPOSITE: This elaborate miniature fondant cake is covered with a removable lace cage made from royal icing and enhanced with delicate royal icing details. One can be served to each guest or used as a topper for a larger cake. Created by Colette Peters of Colette's Cakes.

The following instructions for three cake designs will give you the basic guidelines necessary to create a beautiful wedding cake. The suggested cakes, fillings, and icings are merely that— suggestions. If you prefer chocolate cake to the suggested yellow cake, or you have other recipes and ideas for fillings or icings, by all means use them. Follow your taste preferences and imagination to create a cake that may be similar to the ones featured here, but in the end will be uniquely yours.

## THREE-TIER SQUARE CAKE WITH FRESH FLOWERS
### FLOWERS DESIGNED BY REBECCA COLE OF COLE CREATES
#### SERVES 150

REBECCA COLE is an internationally acclaimed garden, floral, and interior designer and founder of Cole Creates. Her love of sunflowers inspired her to create this simple country wedding cake, but the design could easily work with other flowers. Just be careful to select nonpoisonous varieties; they should be fresh from your garden or from another source that doesn't use chemical sprays. (You can consult with a florist or horticulturist to confirm which flowers are safe to use.) Remove all the flowers before cutting and serving the cake.

The three tiers of this cake can be filled, iced, and boxed separately, then transported to the reception where you can quickly assemble them on-site. In this design, Rebecca secured the flowers by placing their stems in between and around the cake pillars. If you want to stick the flowers directly into the cake, first attach a length of florist wire the same length as the stem and secure it by wrapping the entire length in florist tape.

| INGREDIENTS | MATERIALS AND DECORATIONS | |
| --- | --- | --- |
| 1 recipe White or Yellow Butter Wedding Cake (page 76) | 12-inch square cake cardboard | florist tape |
| 1 recipe Simple Syrup flavored with orange extract (page 80) | 9-inch square cake cardboard | florist wire |
| 6 recipes Chocolate Ganache Icing (page 83) | 6-inch square cake cardboard | heavy duty scissors or |
| 3 quarts fresh sliced strawberries | double-sided adhesive tape | pruning shears |
| | 14-inch square cake board | 2 dozen small sunflowers, |
| | eight 9-inch pillar cake | with the petals removed |
| | separators | 3 dozen fritillaria |
| | 9-inch square separator plate | 4 bunches fresh dill, in bloom |
| | 6-inch square separator plate | |

ASSEMBLY

1. Prepare the Tiers: After the cakes have cooled, slice the layers, moisten with the syrup, and fill with two recipes of the ganache, following the instructions on page 70; sprinkle sliced strawberries in a single layer over each application of ganache filling, gently pressing the strawberries into the ganache with your fingertips. Crumb coat each cake with 4 to 6 cups of the ganache and refrigerate until the crumb coating has set (about 45 minutes). Remove the tiers from the refrigerator, one at a time, and ice with the remainder of the ganache. (See page 71 for tips about working with icing.) Box and refrigerate each tier separately.

2. Insert the Cake Pillars: Position several strips of double-sided adhesive tape on the 14-inch cake board and center the 12-inch cake on the board. Take four of the cake pillars and attach them to the 9-inch square separator plate. Hold the plate in both hands with the pillars facing down, center the pillars over the 12-inch cake, and gently thrust them down into the base cake until the pillars touch the cake board. Gently remove the plate. (There will be approximately 3 inches of the pillars sticking above the top of the cake.)

3. Next, take the 6-inch separator plate and attach the remaining four pillars. Center the pillars over the 9-inch cake, and gently thrust the pillars down into the cake, making sure to touch the bottom cake cardboard. Carefully remove the plastic plate, and set aside the cake and the separator plate.

4. Decorate with Flowers: Place flowers in between and around the cake pillars on the 12-inch cake, using a mixture of sunflowers, fritillaria, and dill. Cut the stems, as necessary, as you work. Alternatively, use florist wire and tape and stick the flowers directly into the cake, as described in the headnote above.

5. Assemble the Tiers: Once you have most of the flowers in place on the first tier, take the 9-inch separator plate and reattach it to the pillars above the 12-inch cake. Place a dollop of icing or double-sided tape in the center of the 9-inch plate,

and place the 9-inch cake, still on its cardboard base, on top of the plastic plate. Decorate the middle tier with flowers, as described in step 4, placing flowers in between and around the pillars. When this is complete, attach the 6-inch separator plate to the pillars sticking out of the 9-inch cake, placing a dollop of icing or a piece of double-side tape in its center. Place the 6-inch cake, still on its cake board, on the separator plate. Decorate the top of the cake with flowers and fill in the other tiers with flowers, as desired.

NOTE: Alternatively, the cakes may be supported with dowels or skewers (see page 71 for instructions). If you choose this method, then use eight 3- or 4-inch pillars, two 6-inch separator plates, and two 9-inch separator plates to separate the tiers. Simply attach the two 9-inch separator plates to each end of four of the pillars and place them between the 12-inch and 9-inch cakes. Likewise, attach the 6-inch plates to the remaining four pillars, and sit this between the 9-inch and 12-inch cakes.

RIGHT: Three-Tier Square Cake with Fresh Flowers; the flowers were designed by Rebecca Cole of Cole Creates.

# PALE PINK FONDANT CAKE WITH CRYSTALLIZED FLOWERS
## DESIGNED BY JOE GILMARTIN
### SERVES 150

JOE GILMARTIN is an accomplished baker and cake decorator who lives and works on the eastern end of Long Island at Tate's Bake Shop in Southampton, New York. Here, he shares one of his beautiful cake designs, artfully decorated with fondant and crystallized flowers. The charming flowers, which are fresh, sugar-coated, and entirely edible, were special ordered from Meadowsweets, a company specializing in candied flowers, based in Middleburgh, New York.

| INGREDIENTS | MATERIALS AND DECORATIONS | |
| --- | --- | --- |
| 1 recipe White or Yellow Butter Wedding Cake (page 76) | 12-inch round cake cardboard | pastry bag and coupling |
| 1 recipe Simple Syrup flavored with framboise (page 80) | 9-inch round cake cardboard | No. 4 round pastry tip |
| 1 recipe Lemon Cream Filling (page 81) | 6-inch round cake cardboard | 10 crystallized pansies |
| 2 recipes Swiss Meringue Buttercream (page 82) | double-sided adhesive tape | 10 crystallized violets |
| 8 pounds white fondant (available at baking supply houses) | 14-inch round cake board | 10 crystallized miniature roses |
| red paste food coloring (available at baking supply houses) | 8 wooden skewers or plastic drinking straws | 2 crystallized daisies |
| 2 cups Royal Icing (page 84) | scissors or pruning shears | |

## ASSEMBLY

1. Prepare the Tiers: After the cakes have cooled, slice the layers, moisten with syrup, and fill with the lemon cream, following the instructions on page 70. Crumb coat each cake with 4 to 6 cups of the buttercream and refrigerate until the crumb coating has set (at least 45 minutes, but up to 3 days). See page 71 for tips on working with icing.

2. Position several strips of double-sided adhesive tape on the 14-inch cake board and center the 12-inch cake on the board. Insert supports into the 12-inch and the 9-inch cakes according to the instructions for supporting the cake on page 71.

3. Cover with Fondant: Work the fondant according to the instructions on page 72 (see also for instructions on coloring). Let all three cakes rest for several hours or overnight to firm up before decorating. The fondant-covered cakes will stay fresh at room temperature for 2 or 3 days. Avoid refrigerating.

4. Assemble the Tiers: Apply a spoonful of the royal icing to the center of the 12-inch cake, then center the 9-inch cake above it and place on top. Repeat with the 6-inch cake, placing it, centered, on top of the 9-inch cake.

5. Decorate the Cake: Put the pastry tip on the pastry bag, and fill three quarters of the bag with royal icing. Pipe a snail-like border around the base of the middle and top tiers, and then pipe a series of small dots onto the cake as shown in photograph opposite. Add the crystallized flowers by placing two or three dots of royal icing in the desired position, then gently press a flower onto the icing.

# WHITE FONDANT CAKE WITH FRESH FRUIT DECORATION
## DESIGNED BY JOE GILMARTIN
### SERVES 100

This is another cake design you can create yourself. The pure white fondant is the perfect background for berries, plums, and fresh herbs, but you can use almost any combination of fresh fruit and even fresh flowers. (Green grapes can be substituted for the Turkish plums if you can't locate any.) I recommend that you box and transport the cake to the reception before decorating. That way the cake can be decorated an hour or two before serving time, so the fruit retains peak freshness and color. This cake design calls for just two tiers, but if you want, you can bake and freeze the 6-inch cake for your anniversary!

| INGREDIENTS | MATERIALS AND DECORATIONS | |
| --- | --- | --- |
| 12-inch round White or Yellow Butter Wedding Cake (page 76) | 12-inch round cake cardboard | 6 large fresh bay leaves* |
| 9-inch round Yellow Butter Wedding Cake (page 76) | 9-inch round cake cardboard | ½ pint fresh red raspberries |
| 1 recipe Simple Syrup (page 80) | double-sided adhesive tape | ½ pint fresh golden |
| 1 recipe Lemon Cream Filling (page 81) | 14-inch round cake board | raspberries |
| 1 recipe Swiss Meringue Buttercream (page 82) | pastry bag and coupling | ½ pint fresh blueberries |
| 6 pounds white fondant (available at baking supply houses) | No. 4 round pastry tip | ½ pint of small green Turkish |
| 2 cups Royal Icing (page 84) | 4 wooden skewers or plastic | plums* |
| | drinking straws | 20 fresh spearmint or |
| | heavy duty scissors or | mint leaves |
| | pruning shears | |

1. Prepare the Tiers: After the cakes have cooled, slice the layers, moisten with the syrup, and fill with the lemon cream, following the instructions on page 70. Crumb coat each cake with 4 to 6 cups of the buttercream and refrigerate until the crumb coating has set (at least 45 minutes and up to 3 days).

2. Position several strips of double-sided adhesive tape on the 14-inch cake board and center the 12-inch cake on the board.

3. Insert the supports into the 12-inch cake according to instructions on page 71.

4. Cover with Fondant: Following the instructions on page 72, roll fondant and cover your 12-inch cake. Repeat for the 9-inch cake. Let the cakes rest at room temperature for several hours or overnight before decorating. The fondant-covered cakes will stay fresh at room temperature for 2 or 3 days. Avoid refrigerating.

5. Assemble the Tiers: When you are ready to decorate the cake, apply a spoonful of the royal icing to the center of the 12-inch cake, then center the 9-inch cake above it and place on top.

6. Decorate Top of Cake: Put the pastry tip on the pastry bag and fill three quarters of the bag with royal icing. As shown in the photograph on page 90, pipe a series of small dots in

groupings of three onto the top edge of both cakes. On the top of the 9-inch cake, place the bay leaves in a pinwheel, with the stems pointing toward the center. Place a drop of royal icing under each leaf to secure it to the fondant. Nearby, create a small mound of red and gold raspberries, adding a few blueberries for color. Position four Turkish plums equidistant around the perimeter of the mound of berries. You should place a drop or two of royal icing on the bottom of each piece of fruit so it will stay put.

*available in specialty food stores

7. Decorate Sides and Bottom Tier of Cake: Place two spearmint leaves, stems pointing towards each other, on the side of the 9-inch cake, and secure with royal icing. Using royal icing to secure each element, position a Turkish plum in the center of the two leaves and accent with a red raspberry, a blueberry, and a golden raspberry (see photo on page 90). Repeat this motif around the perimeter of the 9-inch cake, and around the base of the 12-inch cake. The royal icing dries quickly and very hard, making it a strong adhesive for the fruit.

**OPPOSITE:** This rose-tiered extravaganza by Gail Watson Custom Cakes is a classic. The cake, covered in white fondant, is adorned with gum-paste rose swags that are colored in very pale shades of yellow and cream.

# THE
# BIG

# DAY

7

When your wedding day finally arrives, all eyes will be on you—your dress, your jewelry, your hair, your flowers. Hours of dressing, makeup, and hair will transform you into a radiant bride. Your cake will have undergone a similar transformation. Baked several days before your wedding, it will have been trimmed, filled, stacked, iced,

piped, and adorned. After yourself, your wedding cake will be one of the most photographed and memorable elements of your wedding day.

Wedding cakes are often designed to fit the style and scale of the room they will be displayed in. Be sure to choose a location where the cake can stand on its own and be admired by your guests. A cake worthy of a grand reception room is usually a very large cake. It should be placed prominently as a centerpiece, but make sure that it doesn't overpower the room itself. Keep in mind, too, that enormous cakes usually require on-site construction, because they are impossible to transport assembled and won't fit through doorways.

## DISPLAYING

Displaying a small cake at the reception entrance for all the guests to admire is a great way to show off its beauty without the cake getting lost in a large space. A small cake can also sit at the main table with the bride and groom.

During the final weeks before your wedding, discuss with your wedding coordinator or reception manager where and how your cake will be displayed. The selected surface, whether it's a table or a sideboard, should complement the cake in both scale and design.

Create a foundation worthy of the cake. If your cake is covered in rosebuds, fresh rose petals strewn about will dress up the table without detracting from the cake. The colors of your table covering can match the shade of the cake's icing or a decorative detail. Fabrics like silk or tulle, which evoke a sense of romance, are elegant table coverings. Or, a simple linen or antique lace tablecloth can provide the perfect contrast.

## CAKE-CUTTING

There are different schools of thought about when you should cut the cake. At traditional weddings, the cake is cut close to

David Frankel

the end of the reception, after your guests have wined, dined, and danced for a while. Etiquette dictates cutting just before dessert at a luncheon wedding, or after you have greeted all of your guests at a brunch or tea reception.

Decide when you want the cutting ceremony to take place, and how you want it done. We've all been to weddings where the bride and groom stuff cake into each other's faces and others where the ceremony is enacted with more dignity and grace. Remember that the cake-cutting is symbolic of your first joint act as a married couple, and that it will forever be etched in your friends and family's minds—as well as on film and video.

Traditionally, after the cake-cutting announcement has been made, the bride and groom make their way to the cake table. Usually, the best man or another member of the wedding party will take this opportunity to propose a toast to the newlyweds, after which the groom places his right hand over the bride's hand and they make the first cut together.

After the ceremonial "bite," which many brides and grooms decide to feed to each other, it is customary for the bride and groom to cut and serve their parents slices of the wedding cake. After this ritual is completed, the caterer or a family member will take over the cake-cutting and serve the slices to your guests.

## SERVING THE CAKE

Today, a wedding cake is often served as dessert following the main course. Couples who choose to wait until the end of the reception to cut the cake will usually serve a different dessert after the meal. If you decide to cut your cake at the end of your reception, you can box a piece for your guests to take home.

## SAVING THE CAKE

Another tradition is to remove and save the top tier of the wedding cake. This part of the cake is carefully wrapped and kept frozen until the couple's first anniversary. Discuss preserving the top tier of your cake with your baker, as it will require some coordination with your caterer. Your baker will be able to provide the necessary materials to pack the cake, and should send detailed instructions on how to remove the top and seal for freezing. Some bakers recommend chilling the top tier in the refrigerator for an hour before packing so that the icing and decorations are firm and set. The most important element is to make sure the cake is tightly sealed to avoid freezer burn. Another option that many bakers prefer is to create a replica of the cake in miniature on your anniversary. You may be so busy on your wedding day that you don't remember the food or the cake, and a fresh cake might be a more delicious reminder of your big day than a cake that's been frozen for a year.

IDE

8

# RESOURCE GUIDE

Finding a baker to create the perfect wedding cake will be easier with the following resources to guide you. This list is a compilation of some of the best wedding cake bakers in the U.S., Canada, Europe, and Australia.

*Asterisked names indicate bakers whose cakes appear in this book.

## WEDDING CAKE BAKERS

### UNITED STATES

#### CALIFORNIA

AMAZING CAKES
Anaheim
714.995.3399

ANDRE'S
Menlo Park
650.328.6756

ARTISAN BAKERS
Sonoma
707.939.1765

BUTTERCREAM BAKERY
Napa
707.255.6700

CAKEWORK
San Francisco
415.821.1333
www.cakework.com

CAKEWORKS
Los Angeles
323.934.6515

CITIZEN CAKES
San Francisco
415.861.2228

DELICES
Walnut Creek
510.935.8070

DONALD WRESSEL
Los Angeles
310.273.2222

*ELEGANT CHEESE CAKES
Half Moon Bay
650.728.2248
www.elegantcheesecakes.com

FANTASY FROSTINGS
Whittier
562.941.6266
800.649.0243

HANSEN CAKES
Los Angeles
323.936.4332

HAVE YOUR CAKE
San Francisco
650.873.8488

I LOVE CHOCOLATE
San Francisco
415.750.9460

JAN'S CAKES
Davenport
831.423.4481

JUST FABULOUS PASTRIES
San Diego
619.285.1220
www.justfabulouspastries.com

KATRINA ROZELLE PASTRIES
Alamo
925.837.6337

Oakland
510.655.3209

LA NOUVELLE PATISSERIE
San Francisco
415.931.7655

LE CHANTILLY
San Francisco
415.441.1506

MARJOLAINE
Los Altos
408.867.2226
650.949.2226

MICHEL RICHARD
Los Angeles
310.275.5707

MONTCLAIR BAKING
Oakland
510.530.8052

NANCY'S FANCIES
San Carlos
650.591.8867

PATISSERIE ANGELICA
Santa Rosa
707.544.2253
www.sonomaweddingcakes.com

PATISSERIES DELANGHE
San Francisco
415.923.0711

PATTICAKES
Altadena
626.794.1128

PERFECT ENDINGS
Napa
707.259.0500

Pinole
510.724.4365

PRIMROSE PASTRIES
Castro Valley
510.885.1744

SCHUBERT'S BAKERY
San Francisco
415.752.1580

STELLA PASTRY
San Francisco
415.986.2914

SWEET LADY JANE
Los Angeles
323.653.7145

SWEET PASSIONS BAKERY
San Jose
408.251.1080

TRUE CONFECTIONS
Mill Valley
415.383.3832

YOU TAKE THE CAKE
Berkeley
510.655.4651

VICTORIA PASTRY CO.
San Francisco
415.781.2015

#### COLORADO

THE CAKERY
Littleton
303.797.7418

OPPOSITE: This magnificent creation boasts octagonal, square, and round tiers, which are covered with lavender, green, and pink buttercream and piped buttercream lilacs. The grass and leaf decorations and pink peony topper are made from white chocolate. Created by Liv and Kaye Hansen of the Riviera Bakehouse.

## CONNECTICUT

CLASSIC CAKES AND
PASTRIES
Manchester
860.586.8202
www.classiccakescm.com

SWEET LISA'S
Cos Cob
203.869.9545
www.sweetlisas.com

## FLORIDA

ANA PAZ CAKES
Coral Gables
305.567.2533

Miami
305.471.5850
www.anapazcakes.com

CAKE DESIGNS BY EDDA
Coral Gables
305.445.4600

Doral
305.418.5000

South Miami
305.666.6999
www.cakedesignsbyedda.com

SWEET TIERS
Palm Beach
561.546.8822

## GEORGIA

ANGIE BENNETT
MOSIER CAKES
Atlanta
404.374.6674

## HAWAII

TIERS OF JOY
Waikiki
808.922.9693

WEDDING CAKES BY
LILLIAN MASAMITSU
Honolulu
808.781.2253

## ILLINOIS

EDIBLE WORK OF ART
Chicago
312.895.2200

ROYALE ICING
CUSTOM CAKES
Oak Park
708.386.4175
www.royaleicing.com

THREE TARTS BAKERY
Northfield
847.446.5444

## INDIANA

CLASSIC CAKES
Indianapolis
317.844.6901

## LOUISIANA

CAROL SCHMIDT
Metairie
504.888.2049

## MAINE

SWEET SENSATIONS
Rockport
207.230.0955
www.mainesweets.com

## MARYLAND

ANN AMERNICK
Chevy Chase
202.537.5855

FANCY CAKES BY LESLIE
Germantown
301.972.0926
www.fancycakesbyleslie.com

## MASSACHUSETTS

CAKES BY LIZ
Edgartown
508.696.8444
www.cakesbyliz.vineyard.net

'CAKES TO REMEMBER
Brookline
617.738.8508

CONFECTIONS
Fall River
508.674.4976

KONDITOR MEISTER
Braintree
781.849.1970
www.konditormeister.com

'SOMETHING SWEET
BY MICHELLE
Worcester
508.795.0223

## MICHIGAN

THE CAKERY
Lansing
517.882.1423

## MINNESOTA

VICTORIA'S FANCY
WEDDING CAKES
Sauk Centre
320.352.2636

## MISSOURI

CRAVINGS
Webster Groves
314.961.3534

## NEVADA

FREED'S BAKERY
Las Vegas
775.456.7762
www.freedsbakery.com

## NEW JERSEY

ISN'T THAT SPECIAL
OUTRAGEOUS CAKES
Hoboken
201.216.0123

'ROSEMARY'S CAKES, INC.
Teaneck
201.833.2417

## NEW MEXICO

JAY'S CREATIVE CONNECTION
Albuquerque
505.898.3366
800.240.1149
www.jayscreativeconnection.com

## NEW YORK

BETH HIRSCH
New York
212.941.8085

BETTY VAN NORSTRAND
Poughkeepsie
845.471.3386
DECORATOR/INSTRUCTOR

'BIJOUX DOUX SPECIALTY
CAKES
New York
212.226.0948
bijouxdoux@usa.net

BUTTERCUP CAFÉ
New York
212.350.4144

'CAKE DECORATING BY TOBA
New York
212.234.3635

CAKES BY WENDY KROMER
New York
212.929.4108

CHANTILLY
Brooklyn
718.859.1110

'CHERYL KLEINMAN CAKES
Brooklyn
718.237.2271

'COLETTE'S CAKES
New York
212.366.6530
www.colettescakes.com

CULINARY
ARCHITECT, INC.
New York
212.410.5474

Port Washington
516.883.7885

CULINARY INSTITUTE
OF AMERICA
Hyde Park
845.452.9600

CUPCAKE CAFÉ
New York
212.465.1530

DUANE PARK PATISSERIE
New York
212.274.8447
www.madelines.net

FOOD ATTITUDE
New York
212.686.4644
www.weddingcakeonline.com

'GAIL WATSON
CUSTOM CAKES
New York
212.967.9167
www.gailwatsoncake.com

HIRSCH BAKING
New York
212.941.8085

JUST DESSERTS
Ithaca
607.272.3718

MAKE MY CAKE
New York
212.932.0833

MARGARET BRAUN
New York
212.929.1582

'MY MOST FAVORITE
DESSERT COMPANY
New York
212.997.5130
SPECIALIZES IN
KOSHER CAKES

'PAYARD PATISSERIE
AND BISTRO
New York
212.717.5252

PETER'S CAKES, INC.
Cedarhurst
516.569.4034

**ABOVE:** A charming gift box–shaped cheesecake by Susan Morgan of Elegant
Cheese Cakes.

'RIVIERA BAKEHOUSE
Ardsley
914.693.9758
www.rivierabakehouse.com

'RON BEN-ISRAEL CAKES
New York
212.625.3369
www.weddingcakes.com

ROSIE'S CREATIONS, INC.
New York
212.362.6069

SCHROEDER'S BAKERY
Buffalo
716.882.8424
www.schroedersbakery.com

SWEET EXPECTATIONS
BAKERY
Thornwood
914.741.2284

'SYLVIA WEINSTOCK CAKES
New York
212.925.6698

'TATE'S BAKE SHOP
Southampton
631.283.9830
www.tatesbakeshop.com

## OHIO

FOUR BAKERS
Bexley
614.231.3900
www.fourbakers.com

JAN KISH
Worthington
614.848.5855

## OREGON

DESIGNER CAKES BY
KATHY KEARNS
Bend
541.318.5488

POLLY'S CAKES
Portland
503.230.1986
www.pollyscakes.com

## PENNSYLVANIA

CAKE AND COOKIES
BY MARIA
Walnutport
610.767.7109

SUD FINE PASTRY
Philadelphia
215.592.0499

## RHODE ISLAND

'SCRUMPTIONS
East Greenwich
401.884.0844
www.scrumptions.com

## SOUTH CAROLINA

ASHLEY BAKERY
Charleston
843.763.4125

JEAN PAUL'S CREATIVE CAKES
Charleston
843.774.6791
www.jpcreativecakes.com

## TENNESSEE

SUSAN KENNEDY CHOPSON
Madison
615.865.2437

## TEXAS

A TASTE OF EUROPE
BY GISELA
Fort Worth
817.654.9494

CLIFF SIMON CAKES
Austin
512.428.9366

DANIEL'S BAKERY
Wichita Falls
940.322.4043

EARLENE'S CAKES
Lubbock
806.745.2230
www.earlenescakes.com

FROSTED ART BY ARTURO DIAZ
Dallas
214.760.8707

LE GATEAU CAKERY
Dallas
214.528.6102

## VIRGINIA

JILLY'S CAKE STUDIO, INC.
Alexandria
703.780.4200
www.jillyscakestudio.com

## WASHINGTON

MIKE'S AMAZING CAKES
Redmond
425.869.2992

## WASHINGTON D.C.

ANDREA WEBSTER CAKES
202.337.4867
www.andreawebstercakes.com

## WISCONSIN

SIMA'S
Milwaukee
414.257.0998

## AUSTRALIA

UNIQUE CAKES
Sydney
028.338.0647
www.uniquecakes.au.nu

## CANADA

BONNIE GORDON CAKES
Toronto, Ontario
416.440.0333
www.bonniegordoncakes.com

## ENGLAND

CAKE ART
Cliftonville, Kent
018.432.95514

THE CAKE SHOP
Oxford
018.652.48691
www.the-cake-shop.co.uk

CAKES BY REBECCA BURY
Meppershall, Bedfordshire
014.628.17027
rebeccabury@mvosper.freeserve.co.uk

CARMEN TARRY
CAKE EXPECTATIONS
Hertfordshire
019.208.72657
www.carmentarry.co.uk

THE CHELSEA CAKE SHOP
London
020.773.06277
naomilinfield@aol.com

DELAFIELDS
Wimborne, Dorset
012.028.26666

DUNN'S OF CROUCH END
London
020.834.01614
www.dunns-bakery.co.uk

EDIBLE ART WEDDING CAKES
London
018.144.59779
www.edibleart.freeserve.co.uk

OPPOSITE: (detail on page 64) The dozens of realistic, handmade sugar flowers that cover this multitiered extravaganza were made several weeks ahead of this cake created by Ron Ben-Israel Cakes.

FIONA MOSELEY
Warwickshire
019.268.82680
*fiona.cherry@pop3.hiway.co.uk*

HEATHER HIGGINS WACKY
WEDDING SCULPTURES
019.028.50949
*www.sweetart.com*

IMAGINATIVE ICING
Scarborough, Yorkshire
017.233.78116
*scarborough@imaginative.demon.co.uk*

JANE ASHER PARTY CAKES &
SUGARCRAFT
London
020.758.46177
*www.jane-asher.co.uk*

LINDA CALVERT CAKES
Brighton
012.734.74739
*lind.calvert@virgin.net*

MARK BROOKE WEDDING &
CELEBRATION CAKES
Mollington, Chester
012.448.51880
*subscriber.scoot.co.uk/mark_brooke*

PAT-A-CAKE, PAT-A-CAKE
London
017.148.50006

SUZELLE CAKES LIMITED
London
018.187.44616

FRANCE

FAUCHON
Paris
01.47.45.6011

FLO PRESTIGE
Paris
01.42.61.4546

LENOTRE
Paris
01.45.02.2121
*www.lenotre.fr*

IRELAND

KELTON WEDDING CAKE
GALLERY CO.
Laois
353.(0)502.61132
*www.irish-weddings.com*

SCOTLAND

A PIECE OF CAKE
Millport, Isle of Cumbrae
0147.553.0089
*bibbeth@mac-d.demon.co.uk*

AULDS BAKERS
Greenock
0147.572.5288

BARRACK CAKE DECORATION
Glasgow
0141.332.7730

CAKES BY GILLIAN
Clydebank
0138.987.8934

CREATIVE CAKES
Glasgow
0141.633.0392

FISHER & DONALDSON
Fife & Kinross
0133.447.2201

THE INCREDIBLE CAKE
COMPANY
Glasgow
0141.639.9086
*incrediblecakes@netscapeonline.co.uk*

MACKINNONS BAKERY
Stornaway
0185.170.2804

MARGARET MCKENDRICK
Markinch
0159.275.8206

SCOTBAKE LTD.
Inverness
0146.371.1357

TOP TIER DESIGNER CAKES
Glasgow
0141.334.4244
*evelyn@toptiercakes.freeserve.co.uk*

## MISCELLANEOUS
## RESOURCES

### CAKE DECORATIONS

The following list provides sources
for cake toppers, gum-paste flowers, crystallized flowers, and fresh
flowers.

BEVERLY CLARK
COLLECTIONS
Waukega, Illinois
800.888.6866
*info@beverlyclark.com*
WEDDING FAVORS,
CAKE TOPPERS

**LEFT:** A blue basket-weave cake filled with gum-paste roses by Rosemary Littman
of Rosemary's Cakes.

'REBECCA COLE
COLE CREATES
New York, New York
212.929.3210
FRESH FLOWER DESIGNS

'COLETTE'S CAKES
New York, New York
212.366.6530
www.colettescakes.com
CAKE TOPPERS

ANNE WARREN
CUPCAKE CAFÉ
New York, New York
212.465.1530
CAKE TOPPERS

'GAIL WATSON
CUSTOM CAKES
New York, New York
212.967.9167
www.gailwatsoncake.com
DECORATING KITS,
GUM-PASTE FLOWERS

MELANIE WALDMAN
IT FIGURES—CARICATURES
IN CLAY
Studio City, California
818.509.0200
itfigure@aol.com
CAKE TOPPERS

MARGARET FURLONG
Salem, Oregon
800.255.3114
www.margaretfurlong.com
PORCELAIN CAKE
TOPPERS, FAVORS

'MEADOWSWEETS
Middleburgh, New York
888.827.6477
www.candiedflowers.com
SUGAR CRYSTALLIZED
EDIBLE FLOWERS

REBECCA RUSSELL
New York, New York
212.255.7530
CAKE TOPPERS

## CAKE DECORATING AND BAKING SUPPLIES

Should you be brave enough to bake
your own or someone else's wedding
cake, you will most certainly need
some special equipment, tools, or
decorations. The following suppli-
ers can equip you with all of your
baking and decorating needs, from
cake pans to fondant.

KITCHEN KRAFTS
800.776.0575
fax: 800.850.3093
319.535.8000
fax: 319.535.8001
www.kitchenkrafts.com

OASIS SUPPLY COMPANY
800.441.3141
800.883.0584
215.245.9800
fax: 215.244.4445
www.oasisupply.com

PARTY CAKES 'N THINGS
757.420.5628
fax: 757.420.8178
www.partycakesnthings.com

PFEIL & HOLING, INC.
800.247.7955
718.545.4600
fax: 718.932.7513
www.cakedeco.com

ROSEMARY WATSON
800.203.0629
973.538.3542
fax: 973.538.4939
www.sugarbouquets.com

WILTON
800.794.5866
630.963.1818
fax: 888.824.9520
fax: 630.963.7196
www.wilton.com

## WEDDING WEBSITE ADDRESSES

There are hundreds of bridal sites
on the web these days, but these
are my favorites. Within these sites

you will find everything you will
ever need to know about planning
a wedding, from bouquet designs
to cake ideas.

www.marthastewart.com
www.modernbride.com
www.theknot.com
www.the-wedding-pages.com
www.the-wedding-planner.com
www.tncweddings.com
www.usabride.com
www.waycoolweddings.com
www.wayoutweddings.com
www.weddingbells.com
www.weddingchannel.com
www.weddingdetails.com
www.weddings.co.uk
www.weddingservices.net
www.weddingspot.com
www.wedding-world.com
www.wednet.com
www.wedseek.co.uk
www.wwwweddings.com

## WEDDING CAKE RECIPES AND DECORATING INSTRUCTIONS

www.epicurious.com
www.ices.org
www.pastrywiz.com

## PICTURE CAPTIONS

**FRONT COVER:** (full view on page 3, detail on page 112) An elegant white fondant cake topped with calla lilies by Gail Watson Custom Cakes. **BACK COVER:** An individual cheesecake wrapped in white chocolate and adorned with violets by Susan Morgan of Elegant Cheese Cakes. **PAGE 5:** Handmade sugar rose by Ron Ben-Israel Cakes. **PAGE 6:** (detail, full view on page 49) This glorious cake is a vision on white. Its creators, Doris Schecter and Amilcar Palacious of My Most Favorite Dessert Company, chose to decorate it with cascades of roses. **PAGE 8:** This delicate creation by Sylvia Weinstock is only twelve inches tall. The cake is iced in pure-white buttercream with pale blue and green accents and is adorned with miniature orange blossoms. **PAGE 60:** Ron Ben-Israel puts the finishing touches on a spectacular fondant cake (full view on page 98). **PAGE 68:** Baker's cake-decorating tools and a vintage bride-and-groom wedding-cake topper, courtesy of Ron Ben-Israel Cakes. **PAGE 74:** Assorted pastry tips. **PAGE 96:** Cutting the Riviera Bakehouse's magnificent wedding cake (full view on page 104).